Sous Vide Cookbook

Sous Vide Cookbook

Prepare Professional Quality Food Easily at Home

Julia Grady

Copyright © 2017 by Dylanna Press
All rights reserved. This book or any portion thereof
may not be reproduced or used in any manner whatsoever without the express written permission of the publisher except for
the use of brief quotations in a book review.

First edition: 2017

Disclaimer/Limit of Liability
This book is for informational purposes only. The views expressed are those of the author alone,
and should not be taken as expert, legal, or medical advice. The reader is responsible for his or her own actions.
Every attempt has been made to verify the accuracy of the information in this publication. However, neither the author nor the
publisher assumes any responsibility for errors, omissions, or contrary interpretation of the material contained herein.
This book is not intended to provide medical advice. Please see your health care professional before embarking on any new
diet or exercise program. The reader should regularly consult a physician in matters relating to his/her health and particularly
with respect to any symptoms that may require diagnosis or medical attention.
All trademarks are property of their respective owners.

Photo credits: Shutterstock

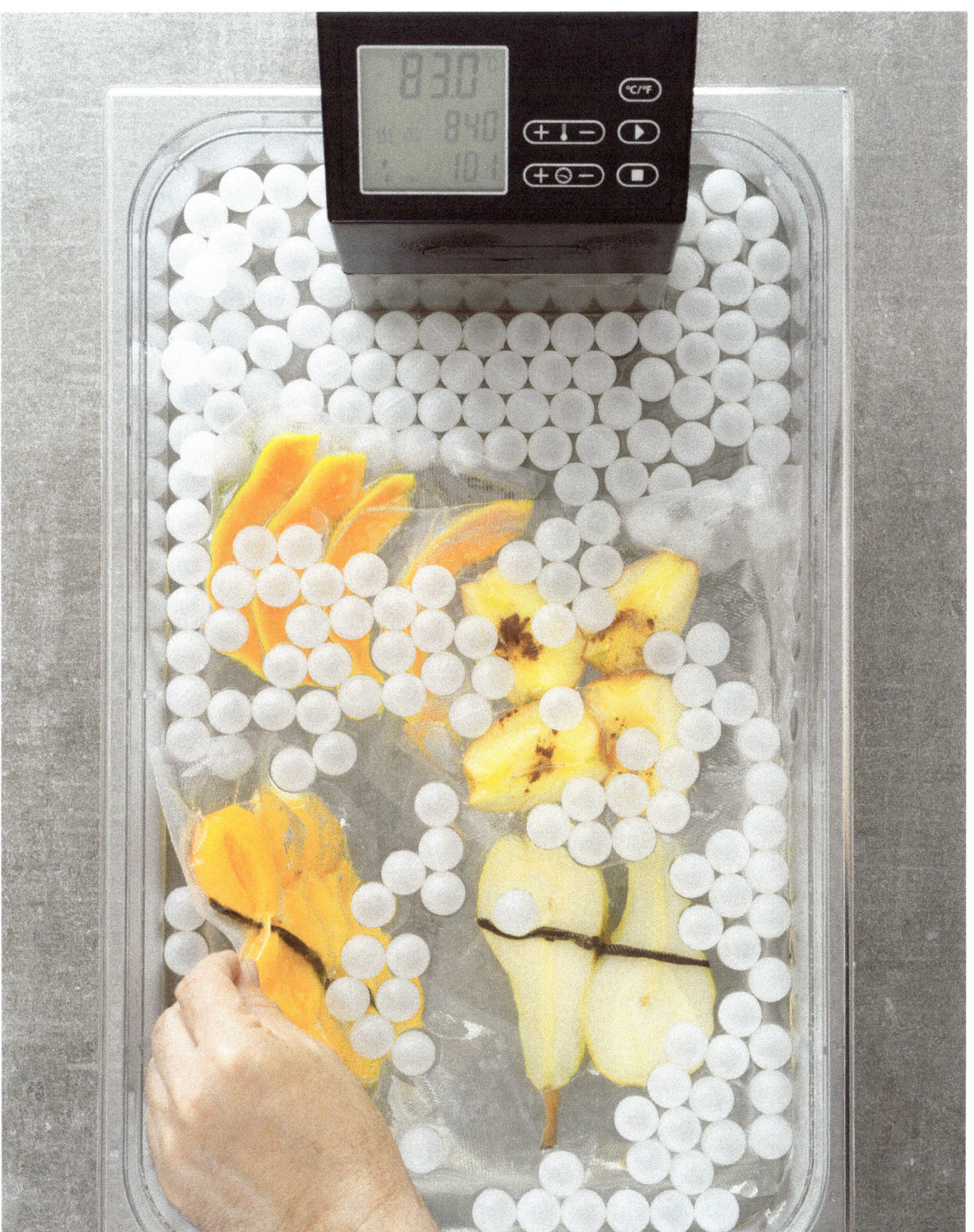

Contents

Introduction 11
The Basics 12
Breakfast 21
- Soft-Boiled and Hard Boiled Eggs 23
- Poached Eggs 24
- Maple Cinnamon Overnight Oatmeal with Cherries 27
- Apple Steel-Cut Oatmeal 28
- Greek-Style Yogurt 30
- Scrambled Eggs 32
- Eggs Florentine with Baby Spinach 33
- Eggs Benedict 34
- Overnight Bacon 36

Beef 39
- Sous Vide Steak 41
- Ribeye Steak with Mushroom Sauce 43
- Beef Medallions in Red Wine Sauce 44
- Smoked Brisket 46
- Flank Steak with Ginger Marinade 47
- Asian-Style Short Ribs 48
- Prime Rib with Horseradish Crust 51
- Caprese Steak Sandwich 52
- Sous Vide Burgers 54
- Italian-Style Meatballs 57
- Steak Tacos 58
- Homestyle Meatloaf 60
- French Onion Meatloaf 62
- Traditional Pot Roast 63

Lamb 65
- Easy, Tasty Lamb Chops 66
- Moroccan-Style Leg of Lamb 67
- Rack of Lamb with Garlic and Herbs 69
- Greek-Style Lamb Meatballs 70
- Spicy Lamb Kabobs 73

Poultry 75
- Sous Vide Chicken Breasts 76
- Spicy Chili Chicken Breasts 77
- Juicy Whole Poached Chicken 78
- Thai Coconut Chicken 80

Spicy Turkey Legs 81
Teriyaki Chicken Wings 82
Curried Chicken 84
Garlic Ginger Chicken Wings 87
Chicken Salad with Mango and Avocado 88
Chicken Fajitas 91
Crunchy-Spicy Chicken Drumsticks 92
Crispy Fried Chicken 94
Southwest Style Turkey Burgers 96
Herbed Turkey Breast 99
Italian-Style Turkey Meatballs 100

Pork 103

Honey Ginger Pork Chops 104
Glazed Pork Chops with Apricot-Mango Salsa 106
BBQ Pork Ribs 108
Asian-style Ribs 111
Crispy Pork Belly 112
Asian-Style Pork Lettuce Wraps 113
BBQ Pulled Pork Sandwiches 114
Chinese-Style Pork Tenderloin 116
Apple Butter Pork Tenderloin 118
Cuban-Style Pork Loin 119

Seafood 121

Simple Sous Vide Salmon 122
Wasabi Salmon Burgers 124
Halibut with Lemon, Coriander, and Scallions 127
Seared Tuna Sous Vide with Mustard-Dill Sauce 128
Orange-Poached Lobster Tails 129
Sea Scallops with Herb Butter Sauce over Linguini 130
Mediterranean Cod 133
Simple Sous Vide Shrimp 134
Shrimp and Avocado Ceviche 135
Soy and Ginger Mahi Mahi 136
Sous Vide Swordfish 139

Vegetables and Sides 141

Cinnamon-Orange Glazed Carrots 142
Eggplant with Spicy Sauce 144
No Mayonnaise Potato Salad 145
Asparagus with Parmesan 147
Mashed Potatoes with Spicy Brown Mustard 148

- Sweet and Spicy Sous Vide Green Beans   150
- Garlic Parmesan Mashed Cauliflower   151
- Cajun Corn on the Cob   152
- Mashed Sweet Potatoes with Truffle Oil   153
- Artichokes Sous Vide   154
- Spiced Quinoa Pilaf   155
- Creamy Mushroom Risotto   156

This and That   159
- Baba Ganoush   161
- Zucchini Pickles   162
- Cranberry Chutney   163
- Spicy Bean Dip   165
- Hummus   166
- Sun-Dried Tomato Infused Olive Oil   168
- Lemon-Infused Olive Oil   168
- Hollandaise Sauce   170
- Chicken Stock   171
- Beef Bone Broth   172
- Marinara Sauce   174
- Sous Vide Limoncello   175
- Blackberry-Infused Gin   176

Desserts   179
- Basil-Infused Peaches   180
- Orange Poached Pears   181
- Egg Custard   182
- Classic Crème Brulee   183
- Creamy Sous Vide Rice Pudding   185
- Cinnamon Ice Cream   186
- Hazelnut Gelato   188
- Lime Curd   189
- Mini Cheesecakes   190
- Spiced Apples   191

Appendices   193

Index   197

From the Author   201

Introduction

Whether you're new to the world of sous vide or have been cooking this way for years, the *Sous Vide Cookbook: Prepare Professional Quality Food Easily at Home* is going to help you make amazingly easy and delicious meals that you and your family and friends are going to love.

Many people arre excited when they first hear about sous vide cooking but aren't really sure where to start. While sous vide is great for cooking steaks and other meats to perfection, it has the potential to be used for so much more.

This books contains a plethora of recipes that have been carefully tested and developed to turn out amazing using the sous vide method. So what are you waiting for?

Happy cooking!

The Basics

Sous vide is a cooking technique that is becoming more and more popular with home cooks. However, sous vide is not new. In fact, it has been used in restaurants since the 1970s but it has only recently been gaining traction at home. This is due to new appliances that have been developed specifically for the home chef. With the help of this new technology everyone can prepare restaurant quality meals easily at home.

What Is Sous Vide?

Sous vide is a French term that means "under vacuum." In this cooking method food is placed in a food-safe bag, vacuum sealed, and then gently cooked in a water bath at a precise temperature, often for long periods of time. Food cooked in this way retains its nutrients, texture, and color better that food cooked by other methods.

Cooking in water in this way is very efficient since water is a better conductor of heat energy than air. Once the food is cooked, it is removed from the water bath and cooking bag, finished by searing, grilling, or another method, and served.

History of Sous Vide

The technique has been around since the mid-1970s when it was developed by two separate cooking pioneers. The chef Georges Pralus of the Restaurant Troisgros in France was trying to find a new way to cook foie gras when he discovered the method. At about the same time in another part of France, Bruno Goussault found that cooking beef in a vacuum-sealed bag in water resulted in a superior tasting meat.

Overview of the Method

Sous vide uses a different approach to cooking than traditional methods. Traditional approaches like baking or broiling use high temperatures to cook food to the desired degree of doneness. For example, if roasting a chicken, you would set the oven temperature to 350 degrees F and cook until the chicken reached an internal temperature of 165 F. While roasting you must keep a careful eye on the chicken so that it does not overcook and become dry and flavorless.

Sous vide is different. With sous vide, the temperature of the water bath is set at the desired temperature of the meat, in this case 165 F. The chicken is vacuum sealed and placed in the water to cook until it reaches the target temperature. Since the water is kept at the desired temperature for the cooked meat, the chicken will never rise above that temperature. It can be kept in the water bath for hours and still be perfectly cooked when removed. The beauty of this technique is that there is no danger of overcooking!

Sous vide is great for cooking all types of meats, steaks, roasts, and poultry. It is also excellent for fish, vegetables, puddings, and more. The recipes in this book will help you unlock the power and versatility of your sous vide machine.

People love the sous vide technique because it is easy, convenient, and virtually foolproof enabling the home cook to turn out amazing, restaurant-quality meals time after time.

How is this different than boiling in bag?

While it may seem similar, sous vide is not really comparable to boiling in a bag. The difference lies in the precise and consistent temperature of the water maintained by the sous vide machine. The water in the sous vide machine never reaches boiling, instead it is kept at the desired food temperature.

Advantages

It may seem at first glance that cooking food sous vide is not worth the time and effort involved. Why not simply throw a piece of steak on the grill and keep an eye on it until it's done – wouldn't that be easier and just as good? Well, not really. Cooking sous vide has many advantages over more traditional methods. These include:

- **Taste** – Cooking at a lower temperature yields juicier, more tender meats and flavorful vegetables. Since the food is vacuum sealed in a bag, it doesn't dehydrate or lose juices while cooking.
- **Consistency** – Cooking with traditional methods can often be hit or miss but the precise temperature control of sous vide cooking means results are reliable again and again.
- **Cost** – With sous vide you can use cheaper cuts of meat and still get tender results.
- **Time** – Since food can remain in the water bath past its cooking time without affecting quality, you can relax and not have to worry about overcooking food.
- **Convenience** – Food can be prepared in advance and cooked slowly in the sous vide appliance, similar to a slow cooker. Sous vide machines can even be set and monitored remotely using your smartphone.
- **Reheating** – Cook food and then store for later use in the freezer or refrigerator. Then just place in the water to reheat.
- **Cook from frozen** – Meat can be cooked straight from the freezer without compromising results.
- **Healthy** – Because of the lower, gentler temperature used during sous vide cooking, many vitamins and nutrients that would be lost using other cooking methods remain intact in the food.

Tools and equipment

Now that you're convinced that sous vide cooking is worth a try you might be wondering what type of equipment is needed. Luckily, there are many appliances on the market today geared for the home cook that make it simple, convenient, and affordable to cook sous vide.

Sous vide machines

In order to cook sous vide you are going to need a way to precisely control the temperature of the water bath. The best way to do this is with an immersion circulator.

Immersion circulators heat and circulate water, keeping the water bath at a uniform temperature. They are a simple and relatively inexpensive solution for sous vide cooking. Popular brands include Sansaire, Anova, and Gourmia. These units clip onto a pot and heat the water to a precise temperature. Many come with Bluetooth and can be controlled using an app on your smartphone.

Next you are going to need a **water bath container**. If you buy a container specially made for sous vide cooking it will be well insulated and come with a lid to help reduce water evaporation. A **water oven**, such as the Sous Vide Supreme has an integrated heating element, and are very convenient. However, they are pricier and will take up a fair amount of counter real estate.

Do-It-Yourself Option

If you just want to try out sous vide before investing in any equipment then it is possible to rig up your own setup. One thing you will need is a digital thermometer to accurately check water temperature. Here are a few DIY options:

- **Use a pot on the stove.** Fill a pot with water on the stove and keep a careful eye on it, adding water as necessary, to maintain a consistent temperature.

- **Use an insulated cooler.** Fill with hot water a couple of degrees hotter than your desired temperature (use hot water from sink and add boiling water from stove until you get to the right temperature). The cooler will hold the temperature pretty stable for several hours. Check often and adjust as needed with additional hot water.

- **Use a slow cooker or rice cooker.** You can purchase an external thermometer that can be hooked up to one of these appliances to keep the water at the correct temperature.

Bags and Sealer

In order to cook sous vide you are going to need bags or other containers to put your food in and a way to seal them so water doesn't get in.

There are a couple of alternatives here. The first is to use **zip-lock bags** and the water displacement method (see page 17) to seal them. This alternative is easy and doesn't require any extra equipment. Make sure you are using food-grade, freezer-style bags (made form polyethylene) that are BPA free. The majority of name-brand food storage bags are considered safe for sous vide.

> **Caution:** At higher temperatures (above about 156 degrees F) the seams on these types of bags can fail. In this case it is best to opt for specialized sous vide bags.

Sous vide bags are specifically designed to withstand higher temperatures and are vacuum sealable. They come in a variety of sizes and are your best option for cooking at higher temperatures.

Canning jars, like mason jars, are another option. These are a preferred option when cooking items such as yogurt, custards, and mini-cheesecakes. Make sure not to overtighten the lids to avoid cracking the glass.

Another useful item is a **vacuum sealer.** There are several styles of vacuum sealer and a range of prices. Vacuum sealing has a couple of advantages over the displacement method. One is it gets more air out and this in turn reduces floating. Also, food that is vacuum sealed can be stored for longer periods of time.

Water displacement method

When you are sealing your bags without a vacuum sealer the best method is the water displacement method, also known as the Archimedes principle. This is a simple technique that uses water pressure to force air out of the bag. Simply place your food into a zip-lock bag and lower the bag into the water bath right up to the seal line. The water will cause the air in the bag to be expelled. Now seal the bag using the zip-lock and you are good to go.

Finishing tools

Sous vide will cook your food to perfection but it will not give it a golden crust or a browned sear. For this you will want to finish your dishes off in a couple of ways, either in a hot pan (such as cast iron) on the stove, on the grill, under the broiler, or using a torch.

Other useful items

- **Tongs** – For removing food from the water bath without burning your fingers
- **Clips and/or weights** – To keep bags from floating
- **Cover for water bath** – Use plastic wrap or plastic balls such as ping pong balls to help reduce water evaporation

Safety

Some people have concerns about the safety of sous vide, whether it be about cooking in plastic bags or the danger of food-borne illnesses when cooking at low temperature. Rest assured that with the proper techniques and precautions, sous vide cooking is very safe.

- **Cooking in plastic**. Always use food-grade plastic bags that do not contain BPA or phthalate that might leach into foods when heated. Name-brand freezer bags are made of polyethylene which is safe for heating. Specialized sous vide bags are also safe for cooking.
- **Food-borne illness.** The USDA considers the danger zone to be temperatures between 40 degrees F and 140 degrees F. Food held for more than two hours at these temperatures can present a risk of growing bacteria which can cause illness. Due to the precision nature of sous vide, you will always no precisely what temperature you are cooking at and can avoid this danger zone. Most immersion circulators and water ovens will warn you if your food is in the danger zone.

- **Botulism.** Another concern is growth of the *C. botulilnum* bacteria which causes botulism. This bacteria can grow in low-oxygen conditions (such as in a vacuum sealed bag). To avoid this, ensure that food does not remain in the danger zone for long by cooking food at correct temperatures and storing properly if not eating right away. Chill food in an ice-water bath to cool it down quickly before refrigerating or freezing.

Sous Vide Basic Techniques

Sous vide cooking is really very simple and this section will break the process down into easy-to-follow steps.

1. **Select the desired temperature** for cooking and preheat the water bath.
2. **Prepare your ingredients**:
    - Pre-sear your meat, if desired
    - Add seasonings
    - Marinate
    - Brine
3. **Place food in bags or jars** — Ensure food is in single layer, this will allow food to cook more evenly. Use multiple bags as needed.
4. **Seal** — Seal using either displacement method or with vacuum sealer. If cooking in jars remember not to overtighten. If steam cannot escape, jars could crack.
5. **Cook in water bath** for desired time.
6. **Remove food** using tongs and finish as desired – searing, grilling, etc. Make sure to pat food dry before searing.
7. **Finishing touches** — Searing your meats and vegetables after removing from the sous vide will yield a delicious brown crust. This needs to be done at high heat. You can use a cast iron pan or other frying pan. Make sure to heat the oil to a high temperature before adding the meat to the pan.
8. **Serve and enjoy!**

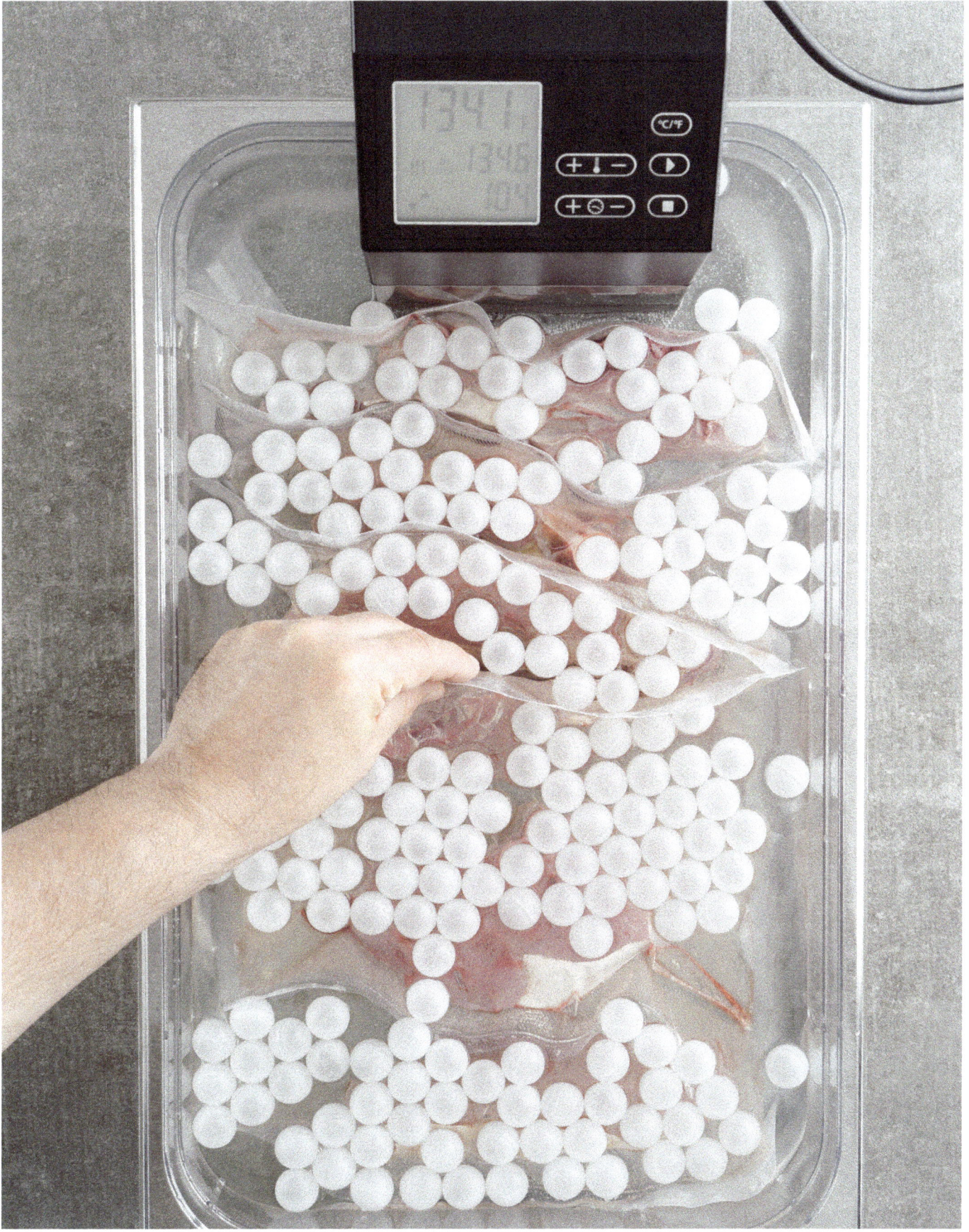

Breakfast

Soft-Boiled and Hard-Boiled Eggs

Eggs are one of the first things most people try sous vide style, and with good reason. The eggshell is watertight so eggs can be placed directly in the water. You will need to do some experimenting to find the perfect temperature for your desired degree of doneness. I like my soft-boiled eggs a medium firmness, still soft but not too watery.

1-12 eggs

1. Fill water bath.

2. Preheat water to 150°F for soft-boiled or 165°F for hard-boiled. (See egg chart below to determine your desired temperature.)

3. Add eggs to the water and cook for 60 minutes.

4. Carefully remove from water using slotted spoon and serve at once. If storing for later use, plunge eggs into ice bath and store in refrigerator for 2-3 days.

Egg Chart

Temperature	Results
140 F	Loose and watery white, very runny yolk
145 F	Loose and watery white, slightly thicker yolk
150 F	Opaque, slightly firm white, tender but firm yolk
155 F	Opaque and firm but tender white with firm yet malleable yolk
160 F	Solid but tender white, firm yolk
165 F	Opaque and firm white, firm moist yolk. Texture of hard-boiled egg

Tip: Make sure your eggs are very fresh.

Poached Eggs

When poached eggs are done right the white is opaque and tight while the yolk is very runny. For the best poached eggs, use the freshest eggs you can find.

....

1-12 eggs

1. Heat water to 145 F.
2. Add eggs and cook for 45 minutes.
3. Carefully remove eggs using slotted spoon.
4. Allow to cool slightly and then carefully crack eggshell and peel away shell. Gently dump egg into small bowl. The egg should be a very soft white and yolk with some watery loose white.
5. With a spoon, scoop out the egg, leaving the loose whites behind.
6. Gently slide eggs into a pan of simmering water, just below boiling. Poach egg for about a minute until egg is set.
7. Remove eggs from pan with slotted spoon and serve.

Note: The eggs can also be stored for later use by submerging in ice bath and then placing in water in refrigerator. When ready to serve, simply reheat in 130-135 F water for 15 minutes or so.

Maple Cinnamon Overnight Oatmeal with Cherries

Servings: 2

1 cup quick-cooking oats

3 cups water

¼ cup maple syrup

¼ teaspoon vanilla

Pinch of salt

¼ teaspoon cinnamon

¾ cup dried cherries

2 tablespoons brown sugar

½ cup water

1. Fill water bath with water and heat to 155 F (68 C)

2. Add oats, water maple syrup, vanilla, salt, and cinnamon to gallon size zip-top bag. Use displacement method (link) to remove air and seal bag. Submerge in water bath.

3. Add cherries, brown sugar, and water to quart size zip top bag. Use displacement method to remove air and seal bag. Add bag to water bath.

4. Cook overnight (6-10 hours). Remove bags from water bath. Pour oatmeal into bowls and top with cherries.

Apple Steel-Cut Oatmeal

Serves: 2

½ cup steel-cut oats
1 large apple, cored and cut into 1-inch pieces
2 cups water or milk
¼ cup honey
¼ teaspoon cinnamon
Pinch of salt
Toppings (optional): Toasted walnuts or pecans, almond butter, raisins

1. Fill water bath with water. Preheat to 155 F (68 C).
2. Add oats, apple, water or milk, honey, cinnamon, and salt to large gallon-size zip lock bag.
3. Use displacement method to remove air and seal bag.
4. Submerge bag in water bath.
5. Cook for 3 hours or for up to 10 hours if cooking overnight.
6. Remove bag from water and pour oats into serving bowls.
7. Stir in almond butter, top with nuts and raisins, if desired.

Greek-Style Yogurt

Making your own yogurt in a sous vide machine is easy and economical.

Servings: 4

1 quart whole milk

3 tablespoons start yogurt with live active cultures (or 3 tablespoons powdered yogurt culture)

1. Pour milk into quart size mason jar and tighten lid. Submerge in water bath and heat to 180 F (82 C). When water reaches desired temperature, allow milk to sit in water for a minimum of 15 minutes. It can stay in longer without a problem since it will not heat above 180 F.

2. Turn temperature down to 110 F (43 C) and allow milk to cool. You can speed this up by adding ice to water.

3. Remove milk from stove and pour into bowl. Allow to cool to 110 F (43 C). You can speed this process up by using an ice bath. Once temperature has cooled to 110 F let milk rest for 15 minutes.

4. Remove jar from water, unscrew lid and stir in active yogurt cultures. Pour milk back into jar or you can use several smaller jars if you prefer.

5. Screw lid(s) on tightly and submerge in water bath. Raise temperature to 115 F and leave in water bath for between 6-24 hours to incubate.

6. Remove jar(s) from water. Layer fine mesh strainer with cheese cloth and place over large bowl. Add yogurt to strainer and allow to drain for 4-6 hours in refrigerator.

7. Spoon yogurt in jar(s) and refrigerate for up to a month.

Scrambled Eggs

Why would you could scramble eggs sous vide when they are so quick in the frying pan? Because sous vide scrambled eggs are so creamy and tender you will say they are worth the wait.

Servings: 2

4 eggs
Sea salt and freshly ground black pepper, to taste
1 tablespoon of butter

1. Preheat water bath to 165 F.
2. Whisk eggs together with the salt and pepper.
3. Pour eggs into sealable bag and add tablespoon of butter.
4. Use the displacement method to remove air from bag and seal.
5. Place bag into water bath and set time for 10 minutes.
6. Carefully remove bag and gently squish bag to break up eggs. Return bag to water bath.
7. Cook for another 8-10 minutes.
8. Remove bag from water and spoon eggs onto plate for serving.

Eggs Florentine with Baby Spinach

A classic breakfast dish made extra healthy with the addition of baby spinach.

Servings: 4

....

4 large eggs
1 tablespoon butter
4 cups baby spinach, washed
Salt and freshly ground black pepper, to taste
Ground nutmeg
2 English muffins, split
Hollandaise Sauce (p. 170)

1. Fill water bath and heat to 148 degrees F.
2. Place eggs in water and cook sous vide for 70 minutes.
3. Heat butter in large skillet over medium-high heat. Add spinach and cook, stirring, until wilted. Season with salt and pepper to taste and remove from heat and set aside.
4. Toast English muffins.
5. Spread dollop of Hollandaise sauce onto each English muffin half and top with spinach. Crack egg onto spinach and top with a little extra Hollandaise sauce. Sprinkle with nutmeg and serve.

Eggs Benedict

The classic morning breakfast.

Servings: 4

....

4 eggs
1 tablespoon butter
4 slices Canadian bacon
2 English muffins, split
Hollandaise sauce (page 170)
Salt and freshly ground black pepper, to taste

1. Fill water bath and heat to 148 degrees F.
2. Place eggs in water and cook sous vide for 70 minutes.
3. Heat butter in large skillet over medium-high heat. Add Canadian bacon and cook for several minutes on each side.
4. Toast English muffins.
5. Spread dollop of Hollandaise sauce onto each English muffin half and top with slice of Canadian bacon. Crack egg on top a spoon a little extra Hollandaise sauce on. Season with salt and pepper to taste and serve.

Variations

Eggs Arnold – Swap the Canadian bacon for smoked salmon.

Eggs Blackstone – Use bacon instead of Canadian bacon.

Overnight Bacon

Bacon cooked sous vide is both crisp and moist. Better yet, it is super convenient. Drop it right in its own bag into the water, cook overnight, and in the morning all you need to do is quickly sear it for a delicious breakfast.

Servings: 4-8

1 pound thick-cut bacon

1. Preheat water bath to 145 degrees F (63 degrees C).
2. Place bag, still in its original vacuum-sealed package, in water bath.
3. Cook sous vide for at least 8 hours and up to 24 hours. Remove from water bath.
4. Heat a large skillet over medium-high heat for several minutes. Add bacon to pan and cook until crisp, 2-3 minutes. Flip bacon over and cook for an addition minute.
5. Transfer to paper-towel lined plate and serve.

Tip

The bacon does not have to be crisped and served immediately. After removing from water bath it can be stored in the refrigerator for a couple of weeks or the freeze for a couple of months. When ready to eat, simply sear in skillet as instructed above. Defrost fully before searing.

Beef

Sous Vide Steak

Many people first get into sous vide cooking because of steak. It is probably the most popular food that is cooked sous vide and it's easy to understand why.

Servings: 2

2 12 oz. steaks, about 1 ½ -inches thick
Salt and freshly ground black pepper
1 tablespoon olive oil
1 tablespoon butter

1. Preheat water bath to the temperature of your choice. See below chart for temperature to doneness guide.
2. Season steak with salt and pepper and seal steaks in vacuum-sealed bag.
3. Place in water bath and cook for 1 hour. If needed, it's okay to leave the steak in the water bath for longer, even up to 4 hours*.
4. Remove from water, unseal, and pat dry.
5. Add oil to cast iron or stainless steel skillet and heat over high heat. When pan is hot place steak in pan and add butter. Sear for 30 seconds, flip steak over and sear for an additional 30 seconds on the other side. Continue flipping and searing one or two more times until desired brownness is reached.
6. Remove from pan and serve.

Variation: Finish the steak on the grill instead of in a pan. Place steak on hot grill and sear on each side until brown crust has formed.

*Food safety note: If cooking your steak to a temperature below 130 F, do not leave in water bath for longer than 2 ½ hours.

Beef Temperature Doneness Chart

Rare	125 F	60 minutes up to 2 ½ hours
Medium-rare	130 F	60 minutes up to 2 ½ hours
Medium	135 F	60 minutes up to 4 hours
Medium-well	145 F	60 minutes up to 4 hours
Well done	155 F	60 minutes up to 4 hours

Ribeye Steak with Mushroom Sauce

This mushroom sauce is a great way to use up the flavorful juices left in the sous vide bag.

Servings: 4

4 (8 ounce) ribeye steaks
Salt and freshly ground black pepper
2 teaspoons plus 1 tablespoon butter
4 sprigs thyme
1 tablespoon olive oil
6 ounces baby Portobello mushrooms, stems removed, sliced
3 cloves garlic, minced
2 shallots, thinly sliced
1 cup beef stock
1 tablespoon Worcestershire sauce
½ cup cream
2 teaspoons Dijon mustard

1. Preheat water bath to desired temperature for doneness. See Beef Temperature Doneness Chart to determine correct temperature.
2. Season each steak with salt and pepper and place into bag. Add ½ teaspoon of butter and sprig of thyme. Seal bags (using either displacement technique or vacuum sealer) and place in water bath.
3. Cook sous vide for 1 hour.
4. Remove steaks from water bath, unseal, and pat dry with paper towels.
5. Add oil to cast iron or stainless steel skillet and heat over high heat. When pan is hot place steak in pan and add remaining butter. Sear for 30 seconds, flip steak over and sear for an additional 30 seconds on the other side. Continue flipping and searing one or two more times until desired brownness is reached.
6. Remove steaks from pan and cover while mushroom sauce is prepared.
7. Lower heat to medium-high and add mushrooms, garlic, and shallots to skillet. Cook, stirring as needed, until mushrooms are softened, about 7-8 minutes.
8. Add beef stock, Worcestershire sauce, and cream. Bring to boil, then lower heat to medium and continue to simmer for about 5-6 minutes until sauce begins to thicken.
9. Remove from heat and stir in Dijon mustard.
10. Place steaks on serving plates, top with mushroom sauce, and serve.

Beef Medallions in Red Wine Sauce

Serve over butter noodles for rich and delicious entrée.

Servings: 4

....

1 1/2-pound beef tenderloin
Salt and freshly ground black pepper
4 tablespoons butter
1 tablespoon olive oil
4 garlic cloves, chopped
3 large shallots, chopped
1 teaspoon dried thyme
1 tablespoon flour
2 cups beef broth (some of this can be the juices left in the bag after sous vide)
2 cups dry red wine

1. Cut beef tenderloin into 12 equal-sized rounds. Season with salt and black pepper.

2. Heat water bath to 140 F or to desired temperature (see Beef Temperature Chart).

3. Place tenderloins in bag(s) and 2 tablespoons of butter, divided equally between the medallions. Seal bags and place in water bath. Cook sous vide for 1 hour.

4. Remove bag(s) from water, unseal, pat medallions dry with paper towel, and transfer to plate.

5. Add oil to cast iron or stainless steel skillet and heat over high heat. When pan is hot place medallions in pan and add remaining butter. Sear for 30 seconds, flip over and sear for an additional 30 seconds on the other side.

6. Remove steaks from pan and cover while red wine sauce is prepared.

7. Reduce heat to medium-high and add garlic, shallots, and thyme and saute for a couple of minutes until soft. Add flour and stir for a minute. Add beef broth and wine. Bring to a boil, reduce heat, and simmer, stirring occasionally, until sauce has thickened, about 10 minutes.

8. Place medallions back in pan, and heat for a minute or two.

9. Transfer medallions to serving plates, top with sauce, and serve.

Smoked Brisket

Brisket cooked sous vide yields a moist and tender brisket that is hard to beat.

Servings: 10

- 1 beef brisket, fat trimmed, about 5 pounds
- ¼ cup coarsely ground black peppercorns
- ¼ cup kosher salt
- 1 tablespoon pink salt
- ¼ teaspoons liquid smoke

1. Combine peppercorns and salt in small bowl. Season meat all over with salt and pepper mixture.

2. Place brisket into large bag and add liquid smoke. If it is too big to fit in one bag, it can be cut in half and placed in two bags. Seal bags using vacuum sealer or displacement method.

3. Allow meat to rest at room temperature for 1 hour.

4. Preheat water bath to 150 F. Add meat to water bath and cook sous vide for 24 to 36 hours.

5. Remove from water bath, unseal and remove from bag, and pat dry with paper towels. Let brisket cool.

6. Brisket can now be finished either in the oven or on the grill. To finish in oven, heat oven to 300 F. Place brisket in pan with wire rack and cook for 2 hours or until it reaches desired level of brownness. If finishing on grill, preheat grill over medium-high heat. Place brisket on grill as far from burner as possible, cover, and cook, flipping once, for about 2 hours, or until it reaches your desired level of brownness. Adjust heat as needed on grill to maintain temperature around 250 F.

7. Allow brisket to rest for 30 minutes. Slice against the grain and serve.

Flank Steak with Ginger Marinade

This recipe is very simple, but oh so delicious.

Servings: 4

....

1 piece of fresh ginger (about 6-inches), sliced into thin slices
1/4 cup sesame oil
8 cloves garlic, minced
2 teaspoons lemon juice
1 tablespoon honey
2 teaspoons salt
1 teaspoon freshly ground pepper
1 tablespoon olive oil
1 1/2 pounds flank steak, trimmed

1. In a bowl, whisk together all ingredients except olive oil and steak. Pour into large resealable plastic bag. Add flank steak, seal, and shake to thoroughly coat steak with marinade.

2. Allow to marinade for 30 minutes at room temperature. Can also marinate in refrigerator for up to 24 hours.

3. Preheat water bath to desired temperature for doneness. See Beef Temperature Doneness Chart to determine correct temperature.

4. Seal bags (using either displacement technique or vacuum sealer) and place in water bath.

5. Cook sous vide for 1 hour.

6. Remove steaks from water bath, unseal, and allow marinade to drip off.

7. Add oil to cast iron or stainless steel skillet and heat over high heat. When pan is hot place steak in pan. Sear for 30 seconds, flip steak over and sear for an additional 30 seconds on the other side. Continue flipping and searing one or two more times until desired brownness is reached.

8. Remove from pan and place on cutting board. Let rest for 10 minutes, slice against the grain into thin slices and serve.

Asian-Style Short Ribs

If you've never tastes short ribs cooked sous vide, you are in for a very nice surprise.

Servings: 8

1 lime, juiced
½ inch ginger, peeled and grated
2 tablespoons sesame seeds
½ cup water or broth
3/4 cup soy sauce or coconut aminos
3 tablespoons sesame oil
1/4 cup honey
6 cloves garlic, minced
1 tablespoons freshly ground black pepper
3 pounds beef short ribs, cut across the bone

1. Preheat water bath to 135 F (for medium ribs) or to desired temperature (see beef temperature chart).
2. In a bowl, whisk together all ingredients except for ribs.
3. Place the ribs into vacuum pouch or resealable bag and pour in marinade.
4. Seal using vacuum sealer or displacement method.
5. Submerge bag into water bath and cook for 36 to 48 hours.
6. Remove from water, unseal bag, and remove from marinade.
7. Ribs can be finished off either by searing in hot pan for a couple of minutes on each side or on the grill.

Prime Rib with Horseradish Crust

Mouth-watering prime rib is wonderful for a holiday feast. Cooking it sous vide means you don't have to worry about overcooking it.

Servings: 6

1 4-6 pound boneless prime rib roast
Sea salt and freshly ground black pepper
1 teaspoon garlic powder
2 sprigs thyme
2 sprigs rosemary
For Horseradish crust:
6 garlic cloves, minced
¼ cup horseradish
2 tablespoons Dijon mustard
3 teaspoons sea salt
3 teaspoons coarsely ground black pepper
2 teaspoons dried thyme
1/3 cup olive oil

1. Preheat water bath to 135 degrees F for medium-rare.

2. Season roast with salt, pepper, and garlic powder.

3. Place in large vacuum pouch or 1-gallon size resealable bag. Add sprigs of rosemary and thyme. Seal bag using vacuum sealer or displacement method and submerge in water bath.

4. Cook sous vide for 8 to 10 hours.

5. About ½ hour before prime is done, preheat oven to 425 degrees F.

6. Make paste by mixing together garlic, horseradish, Dijon mustard, sea salt, black pepper, thyme, and olive oil in small bowl. Set aside.

7. Take prime rib out of water bath, open bag and remove prime rib. Pat dry with paper towel and then place in roasting pan. Rub paste all over prime rib. Place pan in oven and roast for 10-15 minutes, or until desired crispness.

8. Remove from oven and allow to rest for 10-15 minutes before cutting.

Caprese Steak Sandwich

A Caprese salad combined with steak makes for an unforgettable delicious sandwich.

Servings: 6

Two 12 ounce steaks (sirloin or strip)
Salt and freshly ground black pepper
1 tablespoon butter
12 slices crusty bread
6 ounces soft herbed cheese
2 large tomatoes, sliced
12 ounces mozzarella cheese, sliced
¼ cup fresh basil, chopped

1. Preheat water bath to 135 F or to the temperature of your choice. See chart for temperature to doneness guide.

2. Season steak with salt and pepper and seal steaks in vacuum-sealed bag.

3. Place in water bath and cook for 1 hour.

4. Remove from water, unseal, and pat dry.

5. Add butter to cast iron or stainless steel skillet and heat over medium-high heat. When pan is hot place steak in pan and sear for 30 seconds, flip steak over and sear for an additional 30 seconds on the other side.

6. Remove from pan and place on cutting board. Allow to rest for 10 minutes and then slice against the grain into thin slices.

7. Place slices of crusty bread on baking sheet and heat in 350 F oven until lightly toasted.

8. Remove from oven and spread herbed cheese on 6 of the slices of bread. Layer with sliced steak, tomatoes, and mozzarella cheese. Return to oven to melt cheese. Remove from oven, sprinkle with basil, and top each half with remaining slice of bread.

9. Serve and enjoy.

Sous Vide Burgers

Cook burgers sous vide produced perfect medium-rare burgers every time.

Servings: 4

1 egg

1 teaspoon Dijon mustard

1 teaspoon Worcestershire sauce

2 cloves garlic, minced

½ teaspoon salt

½ teaspoon ground black pepper

1 pound ground beef (sirloin preferred)

4 sesame seed hamburger buns

Toppings: Your choice of caramelized onions, sautéed mushrooms, bacon, sliced red onions, fresh tomatoes, cheddar cheese, or whatever you prefer

1. Preheat water bath to 133 degrees F.
2. In a bowl, whisk together egg, Dijon mustard, Worcestershire sauce, salt, and pepper. Add in ground beef and mix gently with hands or fork.
3. Gently shape into 4 equal size patties 1-inch thick.
4. Place each patty into its own bag or pouch and vacuum seal.
5. Submerge bags in water bath and cook sous vide for 2 to 4 hours.
6. Remove from water bath, remove from pouches, and pat dry.
7. Burgers can either be finished on the grill or on stove. To finish on stove, add a little olive oil to pan and heat over medium-high heat. Add burgers and sear for about a minute on each side until browned.
8. Serve on buns, topped with your choice of toppings.

Italian-Style Meatballs

Servings: 4

....

1 pound ground beef
½ teaspoon salt
½ teaspoon onion salt
½ teaspoon garlic powder
1 1/2 teaspoon Italian seasoning
1 teaspoon dried oregano
¾ teaspoon crushed red pepper flakes
2 tablespoons Worcestershire sauce
1 egg, lightly beaten
¼ cup milk
¼ cup Parmesan cheese
½ cup bread crumbs, panko-style
1 tablespoon olive oil

1. Preheat water bath to 140 degrees F.
2. Place ground beef in large bowl and add salt, onion salt, garlic powder, Italian seasoning, oregano, red pepper flakes, and Worcestershire sauce. Mix well to combine. Add egg, milk, Parmesan cheese, and breadcrumbs. Mix until evenly blended
3. Form into 1 ½ -inch meatballs. Place meatballs into resealable bags (4-6 per bag) in single layer. Seal using displacement method.
4. Place bags in water bath and cook for 2 hours.
5. Remove from water bath and remove meatballs from bags. Pat dry.
6. Heat olive oil in large skillet over medium-high heat. Add meatballs and sear, turning to brown all sides.
7. Serve meatballs over pasta with your favorite sauce.

Steak Tacos

These are authentic Mexican-style tacos.

Servings: 6

Two 10 ounce sirloin steaks
1/4 teaspoon salt
Freshly ground black pepper, to taste
1 tablespoon plus 2 teaspoons olive oil
12 (6-inch) tortillas
1/2 red onion, diced
3 fresh jalapeno peppers, seeded and chopped
1/2 bunch fresh cilantro, chopped
3 limes, cut into wedges

1. Preheat water bath to 135 F or to the temperature of your choice. See chart for temperature to doneness guide.

2. Season steak with salt and pepper and seal steaks in vacuum-sealed bag.

3. Place in water bath and cook for 1 hour.

4. Remove from water, unseal, and pat dry.

5. Add oil to cast iron or stainless steel skillet and heat over medium-high heat. When pan is hot place steaks in pan and sear for 30 seconds, flip steak over and sear for an additional 30 seconds on the other side.

6. Remove from pan and place on cutting board. Allow to rest for 10 minutes and then slice against the grain into thin slices.

7. In same skillet, add 2 more teaspoons olive oil and allow to get hot. Add tortillas, one at a time, and cook turning once, until tortilla is lightly browned but still flexible.

8. To assemble tacos, place tortilla on a plate and top with steak, onion, jalapeno peppers, and cilantro. Squeeze lime juice over top.

Homestyle Meatloaf

Comfort food at its best.

Servings: 4

....

1 tablespoon olive oil

1 large yellow onion, diced

3 garlic cloves, minced

¾ pound ground beef

¾ pound ground pork

2 tablespoons tomato paste

1/2 cup bread crumbs

2 large eggs

1 tablespoon oregano

Salt and freshly ground black pepper, to taste

1 can (8 ounce) tomato sauce

½ cup shredded mozzarella cheese

1. Preheat water bath to 140 degrees F.

2. In a medium pan, heat olive oil over medium-high heat. Add onion and garlic and sauté for 3-4 minutes. Remove from heat and set aside.

3. In a large bowl, combine ground beef, ground pork, onion mixture, tomato paste, bread crumbs, eggs, oregano, salt, and pepper. Mix together with fork.

4. Shape into loaf and place in large resealable bag. Use the displacement method to seal. Immerse in water bath and cook sous vide for 3 hours.

5. Heat oven to 425 degrees F.

6. Remove meatloaf from water bath, remove from bag, and pat dry. Place in shallow baking dish, and pour tomato sauce over loaf. Sprinkle with shredded cheese.

7. Place in oven and cook for about 5 minutes, until cheese is melted.

French Onion Meatloaf

Another take on the classic dish.

Servings: 6

---

2 pounds lean ground beef
1/2 cup rolled oats
1/2 cup panko bread crumbs
½ onion, finely chopped
2 eggs, lightly beaten
1 can (10.5 oz.) French onion soup
1 teaspoon dried thyme
1/2 teaspoon ground black pepper
1 cup shredded Swiss or gruyere cheese
¼ cup grated Parmesan cheese
1 can crispy fried onions

1. Preheat water bath to 140 degrees F.
2. In a large bowl, combine beef, oats, bread crumbs, onion, eggs, French onion soup, thyme, and black pepper until well mixed.
3. Form into loaf and place in large resealable bag. Use the displacement method to seal. Immerse in water bath and cook sous vide for 3 hours.
4. Heat oven to 425 degrees F.
5. Remove meatloaf from water bath, remove from bag, and pat dry. Place in shallow baking dish, topped with shredded cheese, Parmesan cheese, and fried onions.
6. Place in oven and cook for about 5 minutes, until cheese is melted.

Traditional Pot Roast

The sous vide method really shines at turning out this traditional favorite.

Servings: 6

One 3- to 5-pound chuck roast
Salt and freshly ground black pepper
¼ cup plus 2 tablespoons olive oil
Springs of rosemary and/or thyme

1. Preheat water bath to 140 degrees F for medium doneness or 132 degrees F for medium-rare.
2. Generously season roast with salt and pepper.
3. Place in large vacuum pouch or 1-gallon size resealable bag. Add ¼ cup olive oil and sprigs of rosemary or thyme.
4. Seal bag using vacuum sealer or displacement method and submerge in water bath.
5. Cook sous vide for 24 to 36 hours.
6. Remove from water, and remove roast from bag. Pat dry with paper towel.
7. Heat 2 tablespoons of olive oil in cast iron or stainless steel skillet over medium-high heat. When hot, add roast and sear on all sides until browned.
8. Remove from pan and allow to rest for 10 minutes before slicing.

Lamb

Easy, Tasty Lamb Chops

Tasty, simple, and delicious. What more could you want?

Servings: 4

2 garlic cloves, crushed
1 tablespoon rosemary, crushed
1 teaspoon thyme
2 tablespoons Dijon mustard
2 tablespoons lemon juice plus additional slices for garnish
3 tablespoons olive oil
4 lamb chops (about 1-inch thick)
Salt and freshly ground black pepper, to taste

1. Preheat water bath to 140 degrees F (for medium lamb chops).

2. In a bowl, combine garlic, rosemary, thyme, mustard, lemon juice, and 1 tablespoon of the olive oil. Stir until well blended. Spread mixture over lamb chops, coating both sides thoroughly. Let marinate for 20 minutes at room temperature.

3. Place lamb chops in bags and vacuum seal. Submerge in water bath and cook for 2 hours.

4. Remove lamb chops from water bath, remove from bags, and pat dry.

5. Heat remaining two tablespoons olive oil in cast-iron or other heavy duty skillet. When hot, add lamb chops and sear for 30 seconds on each side. Serve garnished with lemon slices.

Moroccan-Style Leg of Lamb

Servings: 6

1 leg of lamb (about 5 pounds)
2 teaspoons paprika
2 teaspoons freshly ground black pepper
2 teaspoons cumin
2 teaspoons coriander
½ teaspoon cayenne pepper
5 cloves garlic, minced
1 tablespoon fresh ginger, minced
2 tablespoons fresh cilantro, chopped
¼ cup olive oil
¼ cup lemon juice

1. Preheat water bath to 135 degrees F for medium doneness.
2. Trim an excess fat from lamb leg. Using a sharp knife, make several shallow cuts around the leg of lamb. This will allow the spices to absorb into the meat better.
3. In a bowl, combine the rest of the ingredients to make a paste. Rub spice paste all over the lamb leg. Place lamb into large bag and seal.
4. Immerse in water bath and cook from 6 to 24 hours. The longer it cooks the more tender it will be.
5. Just before lamb is ready, preheat oven to 450 degrees F.
6. Remove lamb from water bath, remove from bag and place on rack in large roasting pan.
7. Place in oven cook for 10-15 minutes or until it reaches desired brownness.
8. Remove from oven and allow to rest for 10 minutes before carving.

Rack of Lamb with Garlic and Herbs

Cooking rack of lamb sous vide ensures you will not be disappointed with overcooked lamb.

Servings: 4

One 4-rib rack of lamb (about 1 ½ pounds)
Salt and freshly ground black pepper
1 teaspoon dried rosemary
1 teaspoon dried thyme
2 garlic cloves, minced
1 tablespoon olive oil
1 tablespoon butter

1. Preheat water bath to 135 degrees F for medium-rare or 140 degrees F for medium.
2. Season lamb with salt, pepper, rosemary, and thyme. Place in bag and add minced garlic. Seal using vacuum sealer or displacement method.
3. Submerge in water bath and cook for 1 hour (can be left in water bath for up to 4 hours).
4. Remove bags from water, remove lamb from bag, and pat dry with paper towels.
5. Heat oil in cast-iron or heavy duty skillet. When hot, add lamb as well as butter and sear on all sides until brown.
6. Remove from pan and allow to rest for 5 minutes before carving and serving.

Greek-Style Lamb Meatballs

Serve these tasty meatballs with a big Greek salad.

Servings: 4

---

1 1/2 pounds ground lamb

2 cloves garlic

1 teaspoon oregano

1/2 teaspoon garlic powder

Salt and freshly ground black pepper, to taste

Zest of 1 lemon

2 tablespoons olive oil

1. Preheat water bath to 140 degrees F.
2. In a large bowl, combine ground lamb, garlic, oregano, garlic powder, salt, pepper, and lemon zest. Mix until evenly blended
3. Form into 1 ½ -inch meatballs, about 16-20 meatballs. Place meatballs into resealable bags (4-6 per bag) in single layer. Seal using displacement method.
4. Place bags in water bath and cook for 2 hours.
5. Remove from water bath and remove meatballs from bags. Pat dry.
6. Heat olive oil in large skillet over medium-high heat. Add meatballs and sear, turning to brown all sides.

Spicy Lamb Kabobs

These lamb kabobs are a flavorful blend of herbs, spices, and garlic.

Servings: 4

....

½ cup olive oil

1/3 cup lemon juice

4 garlic cloves, minced

1 teaspoon ground coriander

1 teaspoon ground cumin

1 teaspoon salt

2 teaspoons ground black pepper

1 ½ pounds boneless leg of lamb, cut into 1-inch cubes

1 red onion, cut into 1 ½-inch chunks

Wooden skewers, soaked for 20-30 in water

1. In a bowl, whisk together olive oil, lemon juice, garlic, coriander, cumin, salt, and pepper. Add lamb cubes to bowl and toss to coat. Marinate for 2 hours or overnight in refrigerator.

2. Preheat water bath to 135 degrees F for medium doneness.

3. Remove lamb from marinade and place in bag(s). Seal and immerse in water bath.

4. Cook for 6 to 24 hours.

5. Remove from water bath, remove lamb cubes from bag(s), and pat dry with paper towel.

6. Thread lamb cubes onto skewers.

7. Sear on hot grill, turning to sear all sides, 1-2 minutes.

8. Serve with couscous or rice pilaf and a green salad.

Poultry

Sous Vide Chicken Breasts

Juicy, tender, and flavorful – chicken breasts cooked sous vide can't be beat.

Servings: 2

2 chicken breasts
Salt and freshly ground black pepper, to taste
2 tablespoons butter
1 teaspoon dried thyme
1 tablespoon olive oil

1. Preheat water bath to 147 degrees F.
2. Season each chicken breast with salt and pepper. Place chicken breasts in cooking pouch or resealable bag and add butter and thyme. Seal bag using vacuum sealer or displacement method and immerse in water bath.
3. Cook sous vide for 90 minutes up to 3 hours. Remove chicken from water bath and bag.
4. Heat olive oil in cast-iron or stainless steel skillet over medium-high.
5. Add chicken breasts and sear about 1 minute per side until golden brown.
6. Serve and enjoy.

Spicy Chili Chicken Breasts

Try this if you like your chicken with a kick.

Servings: 4

- 4 chicken breasts
- ½ cup low-sodium soy sauce
- 2 tablespoons olive oil, divided
- 1 ½ teaspoons curry powder
- ½ teaspoon onion powder
- 1 teaspoon cayenne pepper

1. Add soy sauce, 1 tablespoon olive oil, curry powder, onion powder, and cayenne pepper to large resealable bag. Add chicken breasts, seal bag, and shake to coat chicken with marinade. Place in refrigerator to marinate for 2 hours or up to overnight.

2. Preheat water bath to 147 degrees F.

3. Remove chicken from marinade and add to cooking pouch or resealable bag. Seal using vacuum sealer or displacement method and immerse in water bath.

4. Cook sous vide for 90 minutes up to 3 hours. Remove chicken from water bath and bag.

5. Heat olive oil in cast-iron or stainless steel skillet over medium-high.

6. Add chicken breasts and sear about 1 minute per side until golden brown.

7. Serve and enjoy.

Juicy Whole Poached Chicken

Servings: 4-6

1 whole chicken (3-4 pounds)
Salt and freshly ground black pepper, to taste
1 onion, chopped
½ lemon
3-4 garlic cloves
1 teaspoon paprika
1 teaspoon dried thyme
4 cups low-sodium chicken stock

1. Preheat water bath to 145 degrees F.

2. Wash chicken and pat dry. Season chicken generously with salt and freshly ground black pepper.

3. Place chicken, along with remaining ingredients in large resealable bag. Seal using displacement method and immerse in water bath.

4. Cook sous vide for 7-10 hours, adding water as needed to replace any that evaporates.

5. Remove bag from water and remove chicken from bag. Remaining liquids in bag can be kept and used for stock.

6. Place chicken in shallow baking dish and set under hot broiler until skin is crispy and browned, about three to five minutes.

Thai Coconut Chicken

Servings: 4

- 2-inch piece of fresh ginger, peeled and sliced thin
- 1 scallion, chopped
- Juice of 1 lemon
- 3 garlic cloves
- 1 cup fresh cilantro, packed
- ¾ cup coconut milk, unsweetened
- ¾ cup pork marinade (Stubb's or similar)
- 1 tablespoon soy sauce
- ¼ cup dark brown sugar, packed
- ½ teaspoon salt
- 2 1/2 pounds boneless, skinless chicken thighs or breasts

1. Preheat water bath to 147 degrees F.
2. Place all ingredients except for chicken into food processor or blender. Pulse several times to combine.
3. Pour marinade into large cooking pouch or resealable bag. Add to chicken to bag, ensuring marinade covers chicken evenly. Seal bag with vacuum sealer or using displacement method. Immerse in water bath
4. Cook sous vide for 90 minutes up to 3 hours. Remove chicken from water bath and bag.
5. Heat olive oil in cast-iron or stainless steel skillet over medium-high.
6. Add chicken breasts and sear about 1 minute per side until golden brown.
7. Serve and enjoy.

Spicy Turkey Legs

Perfect for when your craving turkey but don't want to roast a whole bird.

Servings: 4

1 quart water
¼ cup salt
2 turkey legs
1 teaspoon chili powder
½ teaspoon paprika
½ teaspoon garlic powder
½ teaspoon onion salt
Salt and freshly ground black pepper
1 tablespoon olive oil

1. Add salt to water and stir to dissolve. Place turkey legs in water, cover, and allow to brine in the refrigerator for several hours.

2. Heat water bath to 150 degrees F.

3. Remove turkey legs from brine and pat dry.

4. Mix spices together in small bowl. Rub mixture over turkey legs. Place in sous vide bag and seal.

5. Immerse in water bath and cook for 6 hours up to 12 hours.

6. Remove from water bath and pat dry.

7. Heat oil in pan over medium-high heat. When hot, add turkey legs and sear on all sides, about 3-4 minutes.

8. Serve and enjoy.

Alternative: Finish the turkey legs in the oven instead of on the stove. Place on baking sheet and roast in 350 degree oven until desired brownness is reached.

Teriyaki Chicken Wings

Servings: 4

½ cup soy sauce
½ cup honey
¼ cup orange juice
2 tablespoons rice vinegar
1 teaspoon arrowroot flour
1 tablespoon fresh ginger, grated
2 cloves garlic, minced
1 tablespoon sesame oil
1 teaspoon red pepper flakes
Oil, for greasing pan
2 pounds chicken wings
Chopped green onions for garnish

1. Preheat water bath to 160 degrees F.
2. Combine all ingredients through red pepper flakes in a bowl, mix well.
3. Add chicken wings to large resealable bag and the pour marinade over wings. Seal bags using displacement method.
4. Immerse in water bath and cook sous vide for 2 hours.
5. Just before taking wings from water bath, heat broiler.
6. Remove wings and place in single-layer on broiler pan or baking sheet.
7. Finish under the broiler for 3-4 minutes or until wings are browned.
8. Sprinkle with chopped green onions and serve.

Curried Chicken

This curry is spicy, but you can tone it down by cutting out the red chilies and it will still taste delicious. Although the ingredient list looks long, it is mostly spices, and this dish is quite easy to prepare.

Servings: 6

- 2 1/2 pounds boneless, skinless chicken breast, cut into chunks
- Salt and freshly ground black pepper, to taste
- 3 tablespoons ghee or coconut oil
- 2 medium yellow onions, chopped
- 1 tablespoon of fresh ginger, finely chopped
- 4 garlic cloves, minced
- 2 15-ounce cans coconut milk, unsweetened
- 2 cups chicken stock
- 2 tablespoons tomato paste
- 4 medium tomatoes, chopped
- 2 teaspoons cinnamon
- 1-2 red chilies
- 2 tablespoons curry powder
- 1/4 cup fresh cilantro, chopped
- Juice of 1 lemon

1. Preheat water bath to 147 degrees F.
2. Season chicken with salt and pepper and add to pouch or resealable bag along with 1 tablespoon ghee or coconut oil. Seal bag and immerse in water bath. Cook for 90 minutes up to 3 hours.
3. Toward the end of the chicken cooking time, make the curry sauce. In large pan, heat remaining two tablespoons of ghee or coconut oil over medium heat. Add onions, ginger, and garlic and cook until onions are soft, about 5 minutes.
4. Add coconut milk, chicken stock, tomato paste, tomatoes, cinnamon, chilies, curry powder, cilantro, and lemon juice. Stir and let simmer on medium low until chicken has finished cooking.
5. When the chicken is done, remove from water bath. Open bag and add chicken along with juices to pan with curry sauce.
6. Simmer for another couple of minutes. Serve chicken curry over rice.

Garlic Ginger Chicken Wings

Another take on spicy wings, this time with the zing of ginger.

Servings: 4

- 1 tablespoon Frank's Red Hot Sauce (or other red pepper sauce)
- 1 tablespoon vegetable oil
- Salt and black pepper, to taste
- 1 ½ pounds chicken wings, cut at joint
- 1/3 cup flour

For glaze:

- 3 garlic cloves, crushed
- 1 tablespoon fresh ginger, minced
- 1 tablespoon Asian chili pepper sauce
- ¼ cup rice wine vinegar
- ¼ cup brown sugar, packed
- 1 tablespoon soy sauce

1. Preheat water bath to 160 degrees F.
2. In a large mixing bowl, combine Frank's Red Hot Sauce, vegetable oil, salt and pepper. Add chicken wings and toss to coat thoroughly.
3. Add chicken wings to large resealable bag along with flour, shake to coat wings. Seal bags using displacement method.
4. Immerse in water bath and cook sous vide for 2 hours.
5. While wings are cooking make glaze. In large bowl, mix together all ingredients for glaze.
6. Just before taking wings from water bath, heat broiler.
7. Remove wings, place in bowl with glaze, and toss to coat evenly.
8. Place wings in single-layer on broiler pan or baking sheet.
9. Finish under hot broiler for 3-4 minutes or until wings are browned.
10. Remove from broiler and serve.

Chicken Salad with Mango and Avocado

This makes a nice light supper on a summer night.

Servings: 4

3 tablespoons olive oil, divided
Juice of 1 lime
1 tablespoon honey
1 teaspoon fresh ginger, grated
4 skinless, boneless chicken breasts
2 mangoes, peeled and diced
2 avocados, peeled and diced
8 cups mixed salad greens
1 tablespoon balsamic vinegar

1. Preheat water bath to 147 degrees F.

2. In a small bowl combine 1 tablespoon olive oil, lime, honey, and ginger.

3. Brush chicken with oil mixture and place chicken breasts in cooking pouch or resealable bag. Seal bag using vacuum sealer or displacement method and immerse in water bath.

4. Cook sous vide for 90 minutes up to 3 hours. Remove chicken from water bath and bag.

5. Heat 1 tablespoon olive oil in cast-iron or stainless steel skillet over medium-high.

6. Add chicken breasts and sear about 1 minute per side until golden brown. Remove from pan and slice into strips.

7. Add salad greens to large salad bowl. Add sliced chicken, mango, and avocado. Drizzle with remaining olive oil and balsamic vinegar.

Chicken Fajitas

Servings: 4

1 tablespoon chili powder
1 teaspoon cumin
1 teaspoon paprika
1/4 teaspoon cayenne pepper
1/4 teaspoon garlic powder
1 teaspoon salt
1 teaspoon ground black pepper
3 tablespoons olive oil, divided
1 1/2 pounds boneless, skinless chicken breast, sliced into strips
2 bell peppers, sliced
1 onion, thinly sliced
8 small tortillas

1. Preheat water bath to 147 degrees F.

2. Combine chili powder, cumin, paprika, cayenne pepper, garlic powder, salt, and pepper in a bowl. Season chicken pieces with spice mix, reserving about 1/3 of seasoning for later use.

3. Place chicken in pouches and seal. Immerse in water bath and cook sous vide for 90 minutes to 3 hours.

4. About 10 minutes before chicken is done, heat 1 tablespoon of oil in pan over medium-high heat. Add peppers, onion, and remaining spice mix. Cook, stirring occasionally, until vegetables have softened, about 10 minutes.

5. Wrap tortillas in foil and place in warm oven to heat.

6. Remove chicken from water bath and pat dry.

7. Heat remaining oil in second pan over medium-high heat. Add chicken strips to hot pan and sear on all sides until lightly browned, about 1-2 minutes.

8. To assemble fajitas, top tortillas with chicken strips, peppers, and onions.

Crunchy-Spicy Chicken Drumsticks

These crunchy chicken legs are so easy to prepare yet so tasty they're sure to become a family favorite.

Servings: 4

- 12 chicken drumsticks
- 3 tablespoons olive oil or coconut oil, divided
- ½ cup flour
- 1 teaspoon garlic powder
- 1 teaspoon paprika
- 1 teaspoon cayenne pepper
- Salt and freshly ground black pepper, to taste

1. Heat water bath to 158 degrees F.
2. Using basting brush, coat chicken with 1 tablespoon olive oil or coconut oil.
3. In a large bowl, combine flour, garlic powder, paprika, cayenne pepper, salt, and pepper.
4. Add drumsticks to bowl and toss until chicken is covered with seasonings.
5. Place drumsticks into pouches or resealable bags (about 4 per bag) and seal. Immerse in water bath and cook sous vide for 1 hour. Remove from water bath, and pat dry.
6. Heat remaining oil in large heavy-duty skillet over high heat. Add drumsticks and sear for about a minute on each side until golden brown. Remove from pan and season with additional salt and ground pepper. Serve hot.

Crispy Fried Chicken

Servings: 4

1 whole chicken, cut into parts (alternatively, you could buy just the parts you prefer, chicken breasts, thighs, etc.)

Sea salt

½ cup flour

½ cup cornstarch

½ cup Panko breadcrumbs

½ teaspoon salt

1 tablespoon seasoning salt (like Lawry's)

½ tsp ground black pepper

2 tsp paprika

1 cup buttermilk

Oil for frying (canola or peanut oil)

1. Preheat water bath to 155 degrees F.
2. Season chicken with salt and place in bags and seal. Immerse in water bath and cook sous vide for 2-3 hours.
3. While chicken is cooking, prepare coating. Combine flour, cornstarch, breadcrumbs, salt, seasoning salt, pepper, and paprika in large bowl. Pour buttermilk into separate bowl.
4. When chicken is done, remove from water bath and pat dry with paper towels.
5. Heat oil in large heavy duty skillet or Dutch oven.
6. Dip each piece of chicken in buttermilk and then dredge in seasoning mix until evenly coated.
7. Fry in hot oil, in batches so as not to crowd chicken on pan, using tongs to turn chicken until golden brown on all sides, about 2-3 minutes.
8. Remove from oil and place on wire rack until all chicken is fried.
9. Serve hot.

Southwest Style Turkey Burgers

Turkey burgers with a spicy kick.

Servings: 4

....

1 ½ pounds ground turkey
2 cloves garlic, minced
¼ red onion, finely chopped
½ red bell pepper, finely chopped
1 jalapeno pepper, seeded and diced
2 tablespoons fresh cilantro, chopped
2 teaspoons ground cumin
1 teaspoon hot sauce
2 teaspoons steak seasoning
2 tablespoons olive oil
4 slices pepper jack cheese
8 slices crusty French bread, or bun, toasted lightly
Salsa, for topping
Lettuce, for topping

1. Preheat water bath to 145 degrees F.
2. In bowl, combine ground turkey, garlic, red onion, bell pepper, jalapeno pepper, cilantro, cumin, hot sauce, and steak seasoning. Form mixture into 4 patties, about ¾-inch thick.
3. Place each patty into separate sous vide or zip lock bag and seal.
4. Immerse in water bath and cook 1 hour up to 3 hours.
5. Remove from water bath and pat dry with paper towels.
6. Heat oil in heavy duty skillet over medium-high heat.
7. Add burgers and sear for one minute per side, until golden brown.
8. Top each burger with slice of pepper jack cheese and cook for an additional minute to melt cheese.
9. Place each burger on slice of French bread or bun, top with salsa and lettuce, and additional slice of bread or bun.

Herbed Turkey Breast

Juicy and flavorful, this is sure to be a hit with your family and friends.

Servings: 6

1 boneless turkey breast, about 4 pounds
3-4 cloves garlic, minced
2 teaspoons dry mustard
1/2 tablespoon dried rosemary
1/2 tablespoon dried sage
1/2 tablespoon dried thyme
2 teaspoons sea salt
1 teaspoon freshly ground black pepper
2 tablespoons olive oil

1. Heat water bath to 145 degrees F.
2. In small bowl, combine garlic, dry mustard, rosemary, sage, thyme, salt, pepper, and olive oil. Brush mixture on turkey breast, spreading evenly.
3. Place turkey in large vacuum or zip lock bag and seal. Immerse in water bath and cook for 3 hours.
4. Remove turkey from water bath and pat dry with paper towels.
5. Heat broiler. Place turkey on broiler pan and sear under broiler for several minutes until golden brown.
6. Allow turkey breast to rest for about 5 minutes before slicing.

Italian-Style Turkey Meatballs

Delicious with tomato sauce over pasta or plain on buttered noodles.

Servings: 4-6

....

1 ½ pounds ground turkey
¼ cup Parmesan cheese
2/3 cup seasoned breadcrumbs
½ teaspoon garlic powder
1/3 cup fresh parsley
1 teaspoon dried oregano
1 teaspoon dried rosemary
1 teaspoon dry mustard
¼ teaspoon salt
½ teaspoon red pepper
¼ tomato sauce
1 tablespoon olive oil

1. Preheat water bath to 145 degrees F.

2. Place ground turkey in large bowl and add all ingredients through tomato sauce. Mix well to combine.

3. Form into 1 ½ -inch meatballs. Place meatballs into resealable bags (4-6 per bag) in single layer. Seal using displacement method.

4. Place bags in water bath and cook for 90 minutes.

5. Remove from water bath and remove meatballs from bags. Pat dry.

6. Heat olive oil in large skillet over medium-high heat. Add meatballs and sear, turning to brown all sides.

7. Serve with tomato sauce over pasta or over buttered noodles.

Pork

Honey Ginger Pork Chops

These pork chops are very flavorful.

Servings: 4

---

4 boneless pork chops
¼ cup cider vinegar
1/3 cup honey
2 cloves garlic, minced
½ teaspoon ground ginger
1 1/2 tablespoons soy sauce
½ teaspoon freshly ground black pepper
2 tablespoons olive oil

1. Preheat water bath to 145 degrees F for medium pork chops. (See temperature chart in appendix for desired doneness temperatures.)

2. In a bowl, combine vinegar, honey, garlic, ginger, soy sauce, and black pepper.

3. Pour into large zipper lock bag and add pork chops, making sure they are in a single layer. Seal bag using displacement method and immerse in water bath. Cook sous vide for 1 hour.

4. Remove pork from bags and pat dry with paper towel.

5. Heat oil in large heavy duty pan over medium-high heat. Add pork chops and sear on each side until browned, about 1 minute per side.

6. Plate pork chops and serve.

Glazed Pork Chops with Apricot-Mango Salsa

These pork chops are so easy to prepare and mouth-wateringly good.

Servings: 4

1/3 cup Dijon mustard

3 tablespoons balsamic vinegar

1 teaspoon cumin

Salt and fresh ground black pepper, to taste

4 pork chops

2 tablespoons olive oil

For the Apricot-Mango Salsa

4 fresh apricots, pit removed, diced

1 ripe mango, peeled, diced

1/4 red onion, diced small

1/4 cup fresh basil, minced

1/4 cup extra virgin olive oil

1 teaspoon cardamom

1. Preheat water bath to 145 degrees F for medium pork chops. (See temperature chart in appendix for desired doneness temperatures.)

2. In a bowl, mix mustard, vinegar, and cumin.

3. Sprinkle both sides of pork chops with salt and pepper. Brush mustard mixture onto pork chops, covering both sides.

4. Place pork chops into large vacuum seal or zip lock bag (use multiple bags if needed to ensure single layer). Immerse in water bath and cook sous vide for 1 hour.

5. While pork chops are cooking, make the Apricot-Mango Salsa. Mix together all salsa ingredients in bowl.

6. When timer for pork chops goes off, remove pork from bags and pat dry with paper towel.

7. Heat oil in large heavy duty pan over medium-high heat. Add pork chops and sear on each side until browned, about 1 minute per side.

8. Top pork chops with salsa and serve.

BBQ Pork Ribs

Tender and delicious.

Servings: 4

- 2 pounds pork spareribs
- 1 teaspoon sea salt
- ½ teaspoon paprika
- 1/8 teaspoon cayenne pepper
- 1/4 teaspoon garlic powder
- Liquid smoke

For BBQ Sauce

- 1/2 cup brown sugar
- 1/8 cup Worcestershire sauce
- 1/8 cup ketchup
- 1/8 cup soy sauce
- 1/4 cup chili sauce
- 2 cloves garlic, minced
- 1/2 teaspoon dry mustard
- 1/2 teaspoon ground black pepper

1. Preheat water bath to 165 degrees F.
2. Cut ribs into serving size portions
3. In a small bowl, mix together salt, paprika, cayenne pepper, and garlic powder. Rub this spice mixture onto pork ribs.
4. Place ribs into vacuum or zip lock bags. Place a couple of drops of liquid smoke in bags. Seal bags using vacuum sealer or displacement method.
5. Submerge in water bath and cook for 12 hours.
6. Mix together ingredients for BBQ sauce in small bowl.
7. Remove ribs from water bath and pat dry with paper towels.
8. To finish ribs in oven, preheat oven to 325 degrees F. Brush ribs with BBQ sauce, place on baking sheet, and cook in oven for 10-12 minutes per side, basting with additional BBQ sauce when turning over.
9. Remove from oven and serve with additional sauce, if desired.

Alternate method: Ribs can also be finished on the grill. Place ribs on preheated grill on medium temperature. Brush with BBQ sauce and cook 10-12 minutes per side.

Asian-Style Pork Ribs

Servings: 6

¼ cup brown sugar
¾ cup low-sodium soy sauce
¼ cup sesame oil
2 tablespoons rice vinegar
2 tablespoons olive oil
Juice of 1 lime
3 cloves garlic, minced
2 tablespoons fresh ginger, minced
1 teaspoon hot pepper sauce
12 boneless country-style pork ribs

1. In a bowl, mix together all ingredients except for pork ribs. Add ribs, cover, and marinate in refrigerator for several hours up to overnight.
2. Preheat water bath to 165 degrees F.
3. Remove ribs from marinade and place in several vacuum or zip lock bags. Reserve marinade. Seal bags using vacuum sealer or displacement method. Place in water bath and cook for 12 hours.
4. Just before ribs are finished cooking, add reserved marinade to saucepan, bring to boil, reduce heat and simmer until sauce begins to thicken.
5. Remove ribs from water bath and pat dry with paper towels.
6. Finish ribs under broiler. Brush ribs with marinade sauce, place on broiler pan, and cook in oven for a couple of minutes per side, basting with additional marinade when turning over.
7. Remove from oven and serve with additional sauce, if desired.

Crispy Pork Belly

Servings: 6

½ pound pork belly, skin removed
½ teaspoon paprika
Sea salt and ground black pepper, to taste
2 tablespoons oil, for frying

1. Preheat water bath to 170 degrees F.
2. Season pork belly with paprika, salt, and pepper. Place in vacuum bag or zip lock bag and seal. Immerse in water bath and cook for 9-12 hours.
3. Remove from water bath, pat dry, and chill pork belly in refrigerator for several hours.
4. Cut chilled pork belly into six equal portion.
5. Heat oil in large skillet over medium-high heat. Place pork belly sliced in skillet and cook until browned on all sides, a couple of minutes per side.
6. Season with additional salt and pepper.

Asian-Style Pork Lettuce Wraps

Servings: 6

....

2 teaspoons salt
2 tablespoons sugar
1 tablespoon grated peeled fresh ginger
2 tablespoons sherry or white wine vinegar
2 tablespoons olive oil
2 tablespoons unsalted chicken stock
½ cup sweet chili sauce
¼ cup sriracha sauce
1 1/2 teaspoons lower-sodium soy sauce
1 (2 1/2-pound) boneless pork shoulder, trimmed
30 Boston lettuce leaves (about 2 heads)
1/4 cup thinly sliced green onions
1 cup thinly sliced radishes
1 cucumber, diced
Lime wedges (optional)

1. Preheat water bath to 165 degrees F.

2. In bowl, mix together salt, sugar, ginger, vinegar, olive oil, chicken stock, chili sauce, sriracha sauce, and soy sauce.

3. Place pork shoulder in large vacuum-seal or zip lock bag. Pour in marinade mixture and seal.

4. Immerse in water bath and cook sous vide for 18 to 24 hours. Add more water as necessary to combat any evaporation.

5. Remove pork from bag and pat dry with paper towels.

6. Place pork on wire rack in roasting pan and roast in 350 degree F oven golden brown, about 30-45 minutes.

7. Remove pork from oven and shred with fork, it should be very tender.

8. To assemble lettuce cups, place shredded pork in middle of each lettuce leaf. Top with green onion, sliced radishes, and diced cucumbers. Squeeze fresh lime juice on top.

BBQ Pulled Pork Sandwiches

Servings: 8

2 tablespoons paprika
1 tablespoon garlic powder
1 tablespoon dry mustard
2 tablespoons sea salt
1 tablespoon brown sugar
1 (2 1/2 pound) boneless pork shoulder, trimmed
1 cup barbecue sauce
8 hamburger buns
Coleslaw

1. Preheat water bath to 165 degrees F.
2. In bowl, mix together paprika, garlic powder, dry mustard, salt, and brown sugar.
3. Rub the pork with the spice mixture and place in a large vacuum seal or zip lock bag. Seal bag and immerse in water bath.
4. Cook sous vide for 18 to 24 hours.
5. When pork is finished cooking remove from water bath and remove from bag.
6. Place in bowl and shred pork with fork. Add barbecue sauce and mix well.
7. To serve, spoon pulled pork onto hamburger buns. Top with additional barbecue sauce if desired and coleslaw.

Chinese-Style Pork Tenderloin

Servings: 4

1 (1 ½ to 2 pound) pork tenderloin
1 tablespoon soy sauce, low sodium preferred
1 tablespoon hoisin sauce
1 tablespoon dry sherry
1 teaspoon fresh ginger, minced
1 teaspoon brown sugar
1 clove garlic
½ teaspoon sesame oil
¼ teaspoon Chinese five-spice powder

1. Preheat water bath to 140 degrees F (or to desired temperature, see chart in appendix).
2. Place pork in large vacuum seal or zip-lock bag.
3. Mix all other ingredients in a small bowl and then pour marinade into bag with pork. Seal bag and immerse in water bath.
4. Cook sous vide for 1 hour and up to 6 hours.
5. Near end of cooking time preheat oven to 375 degrees F.
6. Remove pork from water bath and place in baking dish. Brush with additional marinade from bag.
7. Bake in oven for 5 to 10 minutes, until pork is browned.

Apple Butter Pork Tenderloin

Servings: 4

- 1 (1 ½ pound) pork tenderloin
- 1/4 teaspoon dried thyme
- 1/8 teaspoon mustard powder
- 2 cloves garlic, minced
- 4 tablespoons soy sauce
- 4 tablespoons sherry wine
- 1 tablespoon olive oil

For the Sauce

- 6 tablespoons apple butter
- 1 tablespoon sherry wine
- 1 tablespoon soy sauce
- 3/4 teaspoon garlic salt

1. Preheat water bath to 140 degrees F (or to desired temperature, see chart in appendix).
2. Combine thyme, garlic, mustard powder, sherry, and soy sauce in large vacuum seal or ziplock bag. Add the tenderloin and seal.
3. Immerse in water bath and cook for 1 hour up to 6 hours.
4. Remove tenderloin from water bath and pat dry.
5. Combine apple butter, sherry, soy sauce, and garlic salt in bowl.
6. Heat oil in heavy-duty skillet over medium high heat.
7. Add pork loin and sear on all sides, about 2 minutes per side. Add apple butter mixture, cook another minute or two until pork is coated and sauce is hot.

Cuban-Style Pork Loin

This works great for making Cuban sandwiches.

Servings: 4

- 4 cloves garlic, minced
- 1 teaspoon salt
- 1 teaspoon ground black pepper
- 1 teaspoon ground cumin
- 1 teaspoon oregano
- 1 teaspoon coriander
- ½ cup orange juice
- ¼ cup lime juice
- 2 tablespoons olive oil
- 1 teaspoon white wine vinegar
- 1 ½ pound pork loin roast

1. Preheat water bath to 140 degrees F or to desired temperature (see chart in appendix).
2. In a large bowl, whisk together all ingredients through white wine vinegar. Add pork loin and seal bag.
3. Immerse in water bath and cook sous vide for 2 hours.
4. Remove pork from bag, reserving marinade. Pat pork dry with paper towels.
5. Pour reserved marinade into small saucepan and simmer over medium heat, stirring occasionally, until it reduced.
6. Heat a little oil in heavy duty skillet over medium-high heat. Add pork and sear on all sides, until browned, about 2 minutes per side.
7. Place pork loin in platter and drizzle with marinade.

Seafood

Simple Sous Vide Salmon

Servings: 4

4 salmon fillets, about 1-inch thick
Sea salt
Your choice of seasonings (fresh basil, thyme, lemon, parsley)
Vegetable oil for searing, if desired

1. Preheat water bath to 123 degrees F.
2. Season salmon with salt.
3. Place salmon fillets in single layer in large zip lock bag (or singly in separate bags).
4. Add seasonings of choice to bags and seal using displacement method.
5. Submerge in water bath and cook sous vide for 40 to 45 minutes.
6. Remove fillets from bag and dry gently with paper towels.
7. Salmon may now be served immediately, chilled and served cold, or pan seared.
8. To sear, heat oil in large heavy-duty skillet over medium-high heat. When oil is hot add salmon (skin-side down if skin on) and sear until browned, about 1 minute. Gently flip and cook on other side for about 30 seconds. Serve hot.

Wasabi Salmon Burgers

Servings: 4

1 pound salmon fillet, skinless

Sea salt

1 egg, lightly beaten

2 scallions, finely chopped

2 tablespoons fresh ginger, peeled, minced

1 teaspoon sesame oil

1 tablespoon olive oil

1/2 teaspoon honey

2 tablespoon reduced-sodium soy sauce

1 1/2 teaspoon wasabi powder

1. Preheat water bath to 130 degrees F.

2. Season salmon with salt.

3. Place salmon in single layer in zip lock bag(s). Seal using displacement method and immerse in water and cook sous vide for 40 minutes.

4. Remove from salmon from bag and gently pat dry with paper towels.

5. Place salmon in bowl and use fork to flake into small pieces. Add eggs, scallions, ginger, and sesame oil and blend well. Form into 4 patties. Cover with plastic wrap and chill in refrigerator for 1 hour.

6. While burgers are chilling, mix together honey, soy sauce, and wasabi powder in small bowl until smooth. Set aside.

7. Heat olive oil in large skillet over medium heat. Add patties and cook until lightly browned, 2 to 3 minutes. Flip over and cook another 2 to 3 minutes. Brush each burger with wasabi mixture and cook another 30 seconds. Serve hot.

Halibut with Lemon, Coriander, and Scallions

Halibut can be very easy to overcook using conventional cooking methods. Cooking it sous vide ensures a beautiful texture.

Servings: 4

....

4 halibut fillets (about 6 ounces each)
Salt
2 tablespoons olive oil
½ cup scallions, chopped
½ teaspoon ground coriander
Juice of ½ lemon
1 tablespoon butter

1. Season halibut generously with salt.

2. Place halibut into zip lock bags, either singly or in single layer in large bag. Drizzle 1 tablespoon of olive oil into bags. Place in refrigerator for about 30 minutes to an hour.

3. Heat water bath to 130 degrees F.

4. Seal bags using displacement method and immerse in water bath. Cook for 30 minutes up to an hour, depending on thickness of fillets.

5. While halibut is cooking, heat 1 tablespoon of olive oil in skillet over medium heat. Add scallions and sauté for 3 to 4 minutes. Stir in coriander and lemon juice and continue to cook, stirring occasionally for another couple of minutes, until scallions are soft. Remove scallions from pan and set aside. Do not wash pan.

6. When cooking time is up, remove halibut from bags and pat dry. Remove skin from fillets if not skinless.

7. Add tablespoon of butter to skillet and heat over medium-high heat. Add halibut fillets and sear for 45 seconds to a minute, until lightly browned. Turn over, return scallions to pan, and heat for another 45 seconds.

8. Remove halibut to plates and top with scallion mixture. Serve immediately.

Seared Tuna Sous Vide with Mustard-Dill Sauce

Servings: 2

2 tuna steaks (1 ½ thick)
Sea salt
Freshly ground black pepper
Juice of ½ lemon
2 teaspoons butter
Oil for searing

For Mustard-Dill Sauce

¼ cup spicy brown mustard
1 teaspoon sugar
1 tablespoon apple cider vinegar
1/3 cup olive oil
3 tablespoons dried dill

1. Preheat water bath to 115 degrees F or to desired temperature (see chart below).

2. Season tuna steaks with salt and pepper, both side.

3. Place in large zipper-lock bag in single layer (or use two bags). Add lemon juice and butter to bag (or divide evenly between bags). Seal bags using displacement method and immerse in water bath. Cook for 1 hour.

4. While tuna is cooking, make the sauce. In bowl, whisk together mustard, sugar, vinegar, olive oil, and dill.

5. Remove tuna from bag and blot gently with paper towel. Season with additional black pepper, if desired.

6. Heat oil in heavy skillet. When hot, add tuna sear for 30 second, turnover and sear on other side for an additional 30 seconds. Serve drizzled with Mustard-Dill Sauce.

Orange-Poached Lobster Tails

Poaching the lobster tails in orange juice add and interesting and delicious flavor.

Servings: 2

- **2 lobster tails, shells removed**
- **6 tablespoons butter, sliced**
- **¾ cup orange juice**
- **¼ cup white wine**
- **2 cloves garlic, minced**
- **½ teaspoon salt**

1. Preheat water bath to 140 degrees F.
2. Place lobster tails, butter slices, orange juice, wine, garlic, and salt into large resealable bag or bags. Seal bags (either water displacement or vacuum seal) and immerse in water bath.
3. Cook sous vide for 1 hour.
4. Remove lobster tails from bag, drizzle with some of the sauce from bag. Serve with additional melted butter and lemon.

Sea Scallops with Herb Butter Sauce over Linguini

Elegant dish that's surprisingly simple.

Servings: 4

....

1 ½ pound sea scallops
Sea salt
Freshly ground black pepper
2 tablespoons butter, divided
1 tablespoon olive oil
1 shallot, minced
1 clove garlic, minced
1/3 cup dry white wine
1 tablespoon lemon juice
½ teaspoon dried thyme

1. Preheat water bath to 122 degrees F.

2. Season scallops with salt and pepper and place in bag(s) in single layer. Add 1 tablespoon of butter and seal bags.

3. Immerse in water bath and cook for 30 minutes.

4. Remove from bags, reserving cooking liquid. Pat scallops dry with paper towels.

5. Heat olive in heavy skillet over high heat. When hot, add scallops and sear for 60 seconds on each side. Remove scallops from pan and set aside while you prepare sauce.

6. Reduce heat to medium and remaining tablespoon butter along with shallot and garlic. Sauté for 2-3 minutes. Add reserved juices from bag, white wine, lemon juice, and thyme. Cook, stirring, until sauce is reduced by half. Remove from heat and add scallops. Serve over linguini or rice.

Mediterranean Cod

Servings: 4

4 cod fillets (6 ounces each)
Salt and freshly ground black pepper, to taste
½ lemon, sliced into thin rounds
2 tablespoons olive oil
¼ red onion, sliced thin
4 plum tomatoes, chopped
1/3 cup Kalamata olives, chopped
1 teaspoon thyme
1 teaspoon basil

1. Preheat water bath to 132 degrees F.

2. Season cod fillets with salt and pepper.

3. Place cod fillets in one or two sealable bags in single layer. Add lemons sliced and 1 tablespoon of olive oil. Seal using water displacement method.

4. Immerse in water bath and cook sous vide for 30 minutes.

5. About 10 minutes before cod is done, heat remaining tablespoon of olive oil in large skillet over medium heat. Add onion and saute for 2-3 minutes. Add tomatoes, olives, thyme, and basil. Continue to cook stirring, for 3-4 minutes.

6. Remove cod from bags and add to skillet along with juices from bag. Simmer on low for an additional 3-4 minutes. Serve hot.

Simple Sous Vide Shrimp

Its easy to overcook shrimp, which is why cooking them sous vide is perfect because you can set the temperature precisely and achieve consistent results. Perfect for shrimp cocktail.

Servings: 4

1 pound shrimp, peeled and deveined
1 tablespoon butter or olive oil
Optional seasonings: minced garlic, shallots, fresh tarragon

1. Heat water bath to 140 degrees F.

2. Place shrimp in large vacuum or zipper lock bag in single layer. Add butter or olive oil and additional seasoning if desired. Seal bags using vacuum sealer or displacement method. Immerse in water bath and cook sous vide for 20 minutes (can be left in water bath for up to 1 hour).

3. Remove from bag and pat dry with paper towel. Chill and serve with cocktail sauce.

Shrimp and Avocado Ceviche

This is a fresh, spicy, summery salad.

Servings: 4

---

2 pounds shrimp, peeled and deveined
¾ cup fresh lime juice
5 plum tomatoes, diced
1 small red onion, chopped
½ cup fresh cilantro, chopped
1 avocado, peeled, pitted, and diced
1 tablespoon Sriracha hot chili sauce
Sea salt and freshly ground black pepper, to taste

1. Heat water bath to 140 degrees F.
2. Place shrimp large vacuum seal or zipper lock bag (use multiple bags if needed so shrimp are in single layer). Seal bags and immerse in water bath. Cook sous vide for 20 minutes.
3. Remove from bags and pat dry with paper towels. Chop shrimp into small pieces.
4. Place shrimp, lime juice, tomatoes, and red onion in a bowl. Mix well to coat everything in lime juice. Cover and refrigerate for about an hour.
5. Remove from refrigerator and add fresh cilantro, avocado, chili sauce, salt and pepper. Mix to combine. Enjoy!

Soy and Ginger Mahi Mahi

Enjoy this Asian-inspired dish over rice.

Servings: 4

2 pounds mahi mahi fillets (4 medium pieces)
2 tablespoons olive oil, divided
2 tablespoons fresh ginger, minced
1 tablespoon garlic, minced
1 tablespoon fresh lime juice
1/4 cup soy sauce
2 tablespoons honey
2 tablespoons dry red wine
1/8 teaspoon cayenne pepper
Salt and freshly ground black pepper, to taste

1. Preheat water bath to 132 degrees F.
2. Season mahi mahi fillets with salt and pepper and place in large sealable bag.
3. In small bowl, whisk together 1 tablespoon olive oil, ginger, garlic, lime juice, soy sauce, honey, wine, and cayenne pepper. Pour into bag with mahi mahi. Ensure fllets are coated with marinade and in single layer. Seal bag using displacement method or vacuum sealer.
4. Immerse bag in water bath and cook for 20 minutes.
5. Remove fish from bag and pat dry. Finish by searing in remaining tablespoon of olive oil, 60 seconds on each side.

Sous Vide Swordfish

Servings: 4

4 (6 ounce) swordfish steaks
Sea salt and freshly ground black pepper, to taste
3 tablespoons olive oil
Juice of two lemons
1 1/2 tablespoons dried dillweed

1. Preheat water bath to 140 degrees F. (This temperature will result in medium done swordfish. Adjust temperature as needed for desired doneness.)

2. Season swordfish with salt and pepper. Place in single layer in large zip-lock or vacuum seal bag (or use multiple bags) along with olive oil, lemon juice and dillweed. Seal bag using displacement method or vacuum seal.

3. Immerse in water bath and cook sous vide for 25 minutes.

4. Remove from bag and blot dry with paper towels.

5. Finish by searing in hot pan with a little oil or on the grill.

Vegetables and Sides

Cinnamon-Orange Glazed Carrots

Cooking carrots sous vide allows them to retain their natural sweetness and bright color.

Servings: 4

1 pound baby carrots, washed
2 tablespoons butter
1/8 cup orange juice
2 tablespoons brown sugar
½ teaspoon cinnamon

1. Preheat water bath to 185 degrees F.
2. Combine carrots, butter, orange juice, brown sugar, and cinnamon in sealable bag. Seal using vacuum sealer or water displacement method.
3. Immerse in water bath and cook for 40 minutes up to 1 hour.
4. Remove carrots from bag and serve immediately or add to hot skillet and saute for 2-3 minutes before serving.

Eggplant with Spicy Sauce

Sous vide eggplant with a delicious spicy sauce.

Servings: 6

4 Japanese eggplants, cut into 1-inch cubes
2 tablespoons olive oil
2 onions, diced
3 garlic cloves, minced
2 tablespoons soy sauce
1 tablespoon rice wine
1 ½ tablespoons oyster sauce
1 teaspoon fresh ginger, grated
1 tablespoon chili garlic
1 teaspoon red pepper flakes
½ teaspoon freshly ground black pepper
Pinch of sugar
1 tablespoon sesame oil

1. Preheat water bath to 185 degrees F.

2. Place eggplant in 1 or 2 large vacuum seal or zip lock bags, in single layer. Seal bags using either vacuum sealer or displacement method. Immerse in water bath and cook for 3 hours.

3. Toward the end of the eggplant cooking time, make the sauce. Heat olive oil in large skillet over medium-high heat. Add onions and saute until they begin to soften, about 2-3 minutes. Add garlic, and cook, stirring, another minute or two. Add soy sauce, rice wine, oyster sauce, ginger, chili garlic sauce, red pepper flakes, black pepper, and sugar. Stir until smooth.

4. When eggplant is done, remove from bags and pat dry on paper towels.

5. Add eggplant to skillet, lower heat, and simmer, stirring occasionally, for 5 minutes.

6. Serve over rice, drizzled with sesame oil.

No Mayonnaise Potato Salad

This nontraditional potato salad features blue cheese and tangy vinegar.

Servings: 6

2 pounds small new potatoes, quartered
2 tablespoons white vinegar
¼ extra-virgin olive oil
1 tablespoon Dijon mustard
2 tablespoons fresh basil, chopped
½ teaspoon freshly ground black pepper
½ teaspoon salt
½ cup red onion, chopped
¾ cup crumbled blue cheese
2 tablespoons fresh chives, chopped

1. Preheat water bath to 185 degrees F.
2. Place potatoes large zipper lock bag in single layer. Seal using displacement method and immerse in water bath. Cook for 90 minutes.
3. While potatoes are cooking, whisk together vinegar, olive oil, mustard, basil, black pepper, and salt in a large bowl.
4. Remove potatoes from bag and pat dry. Add to bowl along with red onion. Toss to coat.
5. Add blue cheese and chives and mix until blended. Refrigerate until ready to serve.

Asparagus with Parmesan

Quick and easy side dish.

Servings: 4

- **1 pound fresh asparagus, ends trimmed**
- **2 tablespoons butter**
- **¼ cup Parmesan cheese, grated**
- **1 teaspoon salt**
- **¼ teaspoon garlic powder**
- **½ teaspoon thyme**

1. Preheat water bath to 185 degrees F.
2. Place asparagus in large zipper or vacuum seal bag. Cut butter into pieces and add to bag along with Parmesan cheese, salt, garlic powder, and thyme. Seal bag and immerse in water bath.
3. Cook sous vide for 12-15 minutes.
4. Remove asparagus from bag and place on serving dish. Pour sauce from bag over asparagus. Season with additional salt and black pepper.

Mashed Potatoes with Spicy Brown Mustard

Servings: 4

1 ½ pounds russet potatoes
2 tablespoons butter
¼ cup milk
Salt and freshly ground black pepper, to taste
¼ cup spicy brown mustard

1. Heat water bath to 185 degrees F.
2. Peel potatoes and cut into chunks
3. Place potatoes in zipper lock or vacuum seal bag(s) in single layer. Add butter and seal using vacuum or displacement method.
4. Submerge in water bath and cook sous vide for 90 minutes.
5. Remove potatoes from bags and place in large bowl. Add milk, salt, pepper, and mustard and mash together. Use electric mixer to whip potatoes until smooth. Add more milk and butter as needed to reach desired consistency.
6. Serve warm.

Sweet and Spicy Sous Vide Green Beans

Asian-style green beans with a kick.

Servings: 4

¾ pound green beans, trimmed
2 tablespoons soy sauce
1 clove garlic, minced
1 teaspoon honey
1 teaspoon garlic chili sauce
2 teaspoons olive oil
Sea salt and freshly ground black pepper, to taste

1. Preheat water bath to 185 degrees F.
2. Place beans, soy sauce, garlic, honey, garlic chili sauce, and olive oil in zipper lock or vacuum seal bag. Shake to mix all ingredients. Seal bag using displacement or vacuum method.
3. Submerge in water bath and cook for 60 minutes.
4. Remove beans from bag and place win serving dish. Season with salt and pepper.
5. Serve and enjoy.

Garlic Parmesan Mashed Cauliflower

A light and tasty alternative to mashed potatoes.

Servings: 4

1 head cauliflower, broken into florets
4 cloves garlic, minced
1 cup chicken broth
2 tablespoons Parmesan cheese, grated
1 ½ tablespoons butter
Salt and freshly ground black pepper

1. Heat water bath to 185 degrees F.

2. Place cauliflower florets into large zipper lock or vacuum seal bag(s) in single layer. Add garlic and chicken broth and seal bags. Immerse in water bath and cook for 1 hour.

3. Remove cauliflower from bag and place in blender or food processor. Add Parmesan cheese, butter, and cooking liquid from bag. Puree until smooth. Season with salt and pepper to taste.

Cajun Corn on the Cob

Cooking corn on the cob sous vide is juicy and flavorful. Adding Cajun seasoning gives it a spicy kick.

Servings: 4

- **4 ears of corn, husked and cleaned**
- **3 tablespoons Cajun seasoning**
- **2 tablespoons butter**

1. Preheat water bath to 183 degrees F.
2. Season corn with Cajun seasoning and place in bag(s) with butter in single layer. Seal bags and immerse in water bath. Cook sous vide for 45 minutes.
3. Remove corn from bags and serve.

Mashed Sweet Potatoes with Truffle Oil

Truffle oil adds and earthy and exotic flavor to the sweet potatoes

Servings: 6

3 large sweet potatoes, peeled and cut into cubes
3 tablespoons butter
1/3 cup milk
½ teaspoon ground ginger
1 ½ teaspoons truffle oil
Sea salt and freshly ground black pepper, to taste

1. Preheat water bath to 183 degrees F.
2. Place sweet potatoes, butter, and milk into vacuum seal or zipper lock bag(s) in single layer. Seal bags and immerse in water bath. Cook sous vide for 2 hours.
3. Remove from bag and place sweet potatoes and liquid from bag into food processor. Add ginger, truffle oil, salt, and pepper. Puree until smooth.

Artichokes Sous Vide

Flavorful artichokes with garlic, butter, and shallots.

Servings: 4

2 artichokes, halved, choke removed
1 teaspoon salt
1 teaspoon freshly ground black pepper
2 tablespoons butter
2 cloves garlic, minced
1 shallot, minced

1. Preheat water bath to 183 degrees F.
2. Season artichokes with salt and pepper and place in zipper lock or vacuum seal bag. Seal bag and immerse in water bath. Cook for 60 minutes.
3. Heat butter in skillet over medium heat. Add garlic and shallots and sauté for 2 minutes. Add artichokes and sauté for an additional 3-4 minutes. Serve hot.

Spiced Quinoa Pilaf

Servings: 4

1 cup quinoa
1 ½ teaspoons curry powder
½ teaspoon salt
½ teaspoon black pepper
½ teaspoon cumin
¼ teaspoon cinnamon
1 ½ cups chicken stock
1 tablespoon olive oil
1 small onion chopped
1 clove garlic, minced
1 (14 ounce) can chickpeas, rinsed and drained
½ cup toasted pine nuts
½ cup raisins

1. Preheat water bath to 180 degrees F.
2. Fill large sealable bag with quinoa, curry powder, salt, pepper, cinnamon, and chicken stock. Seal bag, immerse in water bath, and cook sous vide for 1 hour.
3. Heat olive oil in large skillet over medium-high heat. Add onion and garlic and sauté until softened, about 4-5 minutes. Add contents of quinoa bag along with chick peas, pine nuts, and raisins. Stir to combine well. Serve warm or chilled.

Creamy Mushroom Risotto

Delicious mushroom risotto cooked in the sour vide yields a creamy dish without having to stand and stir at the stove.

Servings: 4

- 1 tablespoon olive oil
- 1 yellow onion, finely chopped
- 2 cloves garlic, minced
- 1 teaspoon fresh parsley, minced
- 1 cup fresh mushrooms, sliced
- Salt and freshly ground black pepper, to taste
- 1 cup Arborio rice
- 3 cups chicken broth
- 1 teaspoon butter
- 3/4 cup grated Parmesan cheese

1. Preheat water bath to 180 degrees F.
2. Heat olive oil in skillet over medium-high heat. Add onion and garlic and saute until tender, 3-4 minutes. Stir in parsley, mushrooms, salt, and pepper. Reduce heat to low and cook, stirring occasionally until mushrooms are soft, about 4-5 minutes.
3. Pour mushroom mixture into large sealable cooking bag and add rice, chicken broth, and butter. Seal bag using displacement method and submerge in water bath. Cook for 60 minutes.
4. Open bag and transfer contents to serving bowl. Stir in grated cheese and serve.

This and That

Baba Ganoush

Servings: 6

2 large eggplants, sliced in half lengthwise

Sea salt, to taste

2 cloves garlic, crushed

Juice of 1 lemon

1 1/2 tablespoons tahini (sesame paste)

1 tablespoons olive oil

1/4 cup fresh parsley leaves

1/2 teaspoon cumin

1/2 teaspoon cayenne pepper

1. Preheat water bath to 185 degrees F.
2. Generously salt eggplant halves and place in single layer in large zip-lock or vacuum seal bag. Use multiple bags as needed. Seal bags using water displacement method or vacuum sealer.
3. Immerse in water bath and cook sous vide for 3 hours.
4. Remove from water bath and remove eggplant from bag. Pat dry with paper towels.
5. Preheat broiler. Place eggplant halves on broiler pan. Broil for 4-5 minutes until browned. Remove from broiler and allow to cool for about 10-15 minutes.
6. When eggplant is cool enough to handle, scrape flesh from each half into food processor. Add garlic, lemon juice, tahini, olive oil, parsley, cumin, and cayenne pepper. Process until smooth. Taste and adjust seasonings as needed.
7. Transfer to bowl, cover, and refrigerate until chilled.
8. Serve with warmed pita bread and crudites.

Zucchini Pickles

An excellent way to use up extra zucchini from the garden

Servings: 6-8

1 ½ cups apple cider vinegar
1 ¼ cups white sugar
1 ½ teaspoons salt
½ teaspoon turmeric
1 teaspoon mustard seed
½ teaspoon celery seed
    1 ½ pounds zucchini, thinly sliced
    ½ onion, thinly sliced

1. Preheat water bath to 185 degrees F.
2. In bowl, stir together apple cider vinegar, sugar, salt, turmeric, mustard seed, and celery seed.
3. Add zucchini and onion slices to large zipper lock bag. Pour vinegar and sugar mixture into bag. Seal using displacement method.
4. Immerse in water bath and cook sous vide for 1 hour.
5. When done, remove immediately from water and place in ice bath to cool.
6. Can be stored in refrigerator for up to two weeks.

Cranberry Chutney

A delicious cranberry sauce that is the perfect accompaniment to turkey.

Servings: 12

4 cups fresh cranberries
1 apple, peeled and diced
½ cup water
½ cup orange juice
¾ cup white sugar
½ cup brown sugar
1 ½ teaspoons ground cinnamon
1 ½ teaspoons ground ginger

1. Preheat water bath to 180 degrees F.
2. Add cranberries, apple, water, orange juice, sugars, cinnamon, and ginger to large zipper-lock bag. Seal using displacement method. Immerse in water bath and cook for 2 hours.
3. Remove from water bath and place in ice bath to cool.
4. Store in air-tight container in refrigerator for up to 1 week.

Spicy Bean Dip

Servings: 6

½ cup dried cannellini beans, rinsed and drained

¾ cup water

1 (7 ounce) jar roasted red bell peppers

1 small avocado, peeled and pitted

2 cloves garlic

¼ cup fresh basil, chopped

1 teaspoon balsamic vinegar

1 teaspoon lemon juice

½ teaspoon sea salt

½ teaspoon freshly ground black pepper

½ teaspoon paprika

½ teaspoon cumin

¼ teaspoon curry powder

2 tablespoons olive oil

1. Preheat water bath to 190 degrees F.
2. Place beans and water in large zipper lock bag. Seal using displacement method and immerse in water bath. Cook sous vide for 3 ½ hours. Drain beans and let cool.
3. Place beans, bell peppers, avocado, garlic, basil vinegar, lemon juice, salt, pepper, paprika, cumin, and curry powder into food processor. Process until smooth. While processor is running, pour in olive oil. Process until smooth.

Hummus

Servings: 4

1 cup chickpeas, soaked overnight
3 cups water
1 mashed garlic clove
1/3 cup of roasted tahini
1/8 cup of lemon juice
3 tablespoons olive oil
1 teaspoon of salt
Parsley (optional for garnish)

1. Preheat water bath to 195 degrees F.
2. Drain chickpeas and place in large zipper seal bag along with water. Seal using displacement method.
3. Immerse in water bath and cook for 3 hours.
4. Remove chickpeas from bag and drain. Add to food processor along with garlic, tahini, lemon juice, olive oil, and salt. Process until smooth. Sprinkle with parsley for garnish.

Sun-Dried Tomato Infused Olive Oil

Perfect for dipping crusty bread.

Servings: 24

10 sun-dried tomatoes, chopped
2 cups olive oil

1. Preheat water bath to 150 degrees F.
2. Add sun-dried tomatoes and olive oil to zipper lock bag. Seal bag and immerse in water bath and cook for 1 ½ to 2 hours.
3. Remove from water bath and strain oil into clean container. Store in refrigerator for up to 2 weeks.

Lemon-Infused Olive Oil

Drizzle over grilled fish, vegetables, or use as a salad dressing.

Servings: 1 cup

1 lemon
1 cup olive oil

1. Preheat water bath to 150 degrees F.
2. Scrub outside of lemon until clean and then dry thoroughly. Use zester, vegetable peeler, or sharp knife to remove the zest (yellow part only, no white pith).
3. Place lemon zest and oil in zipper lock bag or sterilized Mason jar and seal. Immerse in water bath and cook for 1 ½ to 2 hours.
4. Remove from water bath and place in ice bath for 15 minutes.
5. Strain oil into clean sealable container. Store in refrigerator for up to 2 weeks.

Hollandaise Sauce

Classic Hollandaise sauce with a little kick.

Servings: 4

1 stick butter
2 egg yolks, beaten
1 1/2 tablespoons lemon juice
1 1/2 tablespoons water
Pinch of salt
1/2 teaspoon ground cayenne pepper

1. Preheat water bath to 155 degrees F.
2. Place all ingredients in large zip-lock bag. Seal using displacement method.
3. Submerge in water bath and cook sous vide for 45 minutes.
4. Pour contents of bag into blender and process until smooth.

Chicken Stock

Homemade chicken stock will ruin you for store bought.

Servings: 14

4 pounds chicken bones
1 large onion, quartered
2 large carrots, chopped
3 stalks celery, chopped
7 cups water
1 bay leaf
1 thyme sprigs
1 teaspoon fresh ginger, grated
Salt and freshly ground black pepper, to taste

1. Preheat oven to 425 degrees F. Heat water bath to 190 degrees F.
2. Place chicken bones, onion, carrots, and celery in roasting pan. Roast for 30 minutes, or until browned. Transfer the bones and vegetables to large zip lock bag.
3. Add water, bay leaf, thyme, and ginger to bag and seal.
4. Immerse in water bath and cook sous vide for 12 hours. Add water as needed to water bath to make up for evaporation.
5. Remove from water bath and strain the stock through a fine mesh strainer into bowl. Discard solids. Season with salt and pepper to taste. Allow to cool before transferring to airtight container. Store in refrigerator for up to 1 week or freeze.

Beef Bone Broth

Sip this bone broth by the mugful to take advantage of its amazing nourishing qualities.

Servings 8

2 pounds beef bones
2 onions, quartered
2 large carrots, chopped
1 tablespoon olive oil
6 cups water
3 cloves garlic
2 bay leaves

1. Preheat oven to 425 degrees F. Heat water bath to 190 degrees F.
2. Place beef bones, onion, and carrots in roasting pan. Drizzle with olive oil. Bake in oven for 30-40 minutes, until beef browns.
3. Transfer bones and vegetables to large zip lock bag. Add water, garlic, and bay leaves. Seal bag using displacement method.
4. Immerse in water bath and cook for 12 hours. Strain stock through fine mesh strainer, discarding solids. Allow to cool to room temperature. Store in refrigerator in airtight container for up to 1 week or freeze.

Marinara Sauce

A rich and flavorful sauce perfect for pasta.

Servings: 6

2 tablespoons olive oil
½ onion, chopped
6 cloves garlic, minced
1 (28-ounce) can whole tomatoes
1 bay leaf
½ cup red wine
2 teaspoons dried basil
1 teaspoon dried marjoram
1 teaspoon salt
½ teaspoon freshly ground black pepper
½ teaspoon crushed red pepper
1 teaspoon honey
2 teaspoons balsamic vinegar

1. Preheat water bath to 190 degrees F.

2. Heat oil in skillet over medium heat. Add onion and garlic and sauté until soft, about 5 minutes. Add to large zipper lock bag along with tomatoes, bay leaf, red wine, basil, marjoram, salt, black pepper, red pepper, and honey. Seal bag using water displacement method. Immerse in water bath and cook sous vide for 90 minutes.

3. Remove from water bath. Pour contents into blender or food processor, removing and discarding bay leaves. Add balsamic vinegar and blend until smooth. Use immediately or store in refrigerator in airtight container for 2-3 days.

Sous Vide Limoncello

Making infused vodka is much quicker using sous vide.

Servings: 1 liter

1 liter vodka
6 lemons
1 cup sugar

1. Preheat water bath to 150 degrees F.
2. Peel lemons, removing only zest and being careful to avoid the bitter pith.
3. Place vodka, lemon zest, and sugar in zip lock bag or mason jar and seal.
4. Immerse in water bath and cook for 2 hours.
5. Strain vodka into clean bottle.
6. Store in refrigerator for 3-4 weeks.

Blackberry-Infused Gin

Servings: 16

16 ounces gin
1 lemon
1 cup blueberries, fresh or frozen
½ cup sugar
1 clove

1. Preheat water bath to 150 degrees F.
2. Peel lemon, removing only the zest and being careful to avoid the bitter pith (white part).
3. Place gin, blackberries, lemon, sugar, and clove into zip lock bag or mason jar and seal.
4. Immerse in water bath for 2 hours.
5. Strain gin into clean bottle.
6. Store in refrigerator for 3-4 weeks.

Desserts

Basil-Infused Peaches

Delicious over vanilla ice cream.

Servings: 4

¾ **cup sugar**
1 cup water
10 fresh basil leaves, chopped
4 fresh peaches, cut into pieces

1. Preheat water bath to 180 degrees F.
2. Combine sugar and water in small saucepan over medium heat. Stir until sugar is dissolved, 3-4 minutes.
3. Remove from heat and stir in basil.
4. Place peaches in zip lock or vacuum seal bag and pour in sugar water mixture. Seal bag and immerse in water bath.
5. Cook sous vide for 45 minutes. Remove from water bath and place in ice bath to cool.
6. Serve over vanilla ice cream.

Orange Poached Pears

Simple and delicious.

Servings: 4

---

1 ½ cups orange juice
¼ cup white sugar
¼ cup brown sugar
`1 tablespoon vanilla extract
1 teaspoon cinnamon
4 fresh pears, peeled and cored
½ cup chopped walnuts

1. Preheat water bath to 175 degrees F.
2. Combine orange juice, white sugar, brown sugar, vanilla, and cinnamon in saucepan over medium heat. Cook, stirring, until sugars dissolve, 4-5 minutes.
3. Place pears in large zip or vacuum bag. Pour orange juice mixture into bag and seal.
4. Immerse in water bath and cook sous vide for 45 minutes.
5. Remove pears from bag and place in serving plates. Pour liquid into saucepan and cook over medium heat until thickened and reduced, about 10 minutes.
6. Pour sauce over pears, sprinkle with chopped walnuts, and serve.

Egg Custard

Sweet and comforting traditional egg custard.

Servings: 6

2 cups milk
2 eggs, beaten
½ cup sugar
½ teaspoon salt
½ teaspoon vanilla extract
½ teaspoon ground nutmeg

1. Preheat water bath to 180 degrees F.
2. In a bowl, whisk together milk, eggs, sugar, salt, vanilla, and nutmeg until well combined. Pour into 6 half-pint mason jars. Screw on lids being careful not to overtighten.
3. Place in water bath and cook sous vide for 1 hour.
4. Remove jars from water bath and place in ice bath for 10 minutes to cool. Chill in refrigerator for up to several days.

Classic Crème Brulee

Servings: 4

½ cup white sugar
6 egg yolks
½ teaspoon vanilla
2 cups heavy cream
2 tablespoons brown sugar

1. Preheat water bath to 180 degrees F.
2. In bowl, whisk together white sugar, egg yolks, and vanilla. Pour cream into mixture and stir. Pour into four 1/2-pint mason jars and screw on lids gently, being careful not to overtighten.
3. Submerge in water bath and cook sous vide for 60 minutes.
4. Remove from water bath and let sit until they are cool to the touch. Transfer to ice bath and chill completely.
5. Serve immediately or store in refrigerator for up to 1 week.
6. When ready to serve, remove lid and sprinkle with brown sugar. Place under hot broiler for several minutes to caramelize sugar.
7. Serve and enjoy!

Creamy Sous Vide Rice Pudding

Delicious and creamy rice pudding.

Servings: 4

---

1 cup short grain white rice, uncooked
2 cups milk
1/3 cup white sugar
1 egg, beaten
2/3 cup raisins
1 tablespoon butter, melted
1 teaspoon vanilla extract
½ teaspoon salt

1. Preheat water bath to 180 degrees F.
2. Combine all ingredients in large zip lock bag. Seal using displacement method and submerge bag in water bath.
3. Cook sous vide for 3 hours. Remove bag from water and divide pudding into serving bowls.
4. Serve and enjoy!

Cinnamon Ice Cream

Make this for a delicious treat!

Servings: 8

1 cup white sugar

1 ½ cups half-and-half

4 egg yolks, beaten

1 cup heavy cream

1 teaspoon vanilla extract

2 teaspoons ground cinnamon

1. Preheat water bath to 180 degrees F.
2. Whisk together all ingredients in large bowl until well blended.
3. Pour into large zip lock bag and seal using displacement method. Submerge in water bath and cook sous vide for 1 hour. Swish bag around a couple of times during cooking to prevent lumps.
4. Remove from water bath and place in ice bath to cool.
5. Pour cooled mixture into ice cream maker and follow manufacturer's directions.
6. Store in freezer until ready to eat.

Hazelnut Gelato

Smooth and creamy with a subtle hazelnut flavor.

Servings: 8

1 cup heavy cream
2 cups whole milk
½ cup white sugar
4 egg yolks, beaten
½ cup chocolate hazelnut spread (like Nutella)
2 tablespoons instant espresso powder
½ teaspoon vanilla extract

1. Preheat water bath to 180 degrees F.
2. Whisk together all ingredients in large bowl until well blended. Alternately, place in blender or food processor and blend for 20-30 seconds.
3. Pour into large zip lock bag and seal using displacement method.
4. Place bag in water bath and cook sous vide for 60 minutes. Remove and transfer to ice bath to cool.
5. Pour mixture through strainer into bowl and place in refrigerator to chill for 3-4 hours.
6. Pour into ice cream maker and follow manufacturer's directions.
7. Freeze until ready to eat.

Lime Curd

A slight twist on traditional lemon curd. Perfect as a topping on Mini Cheesecakes.

Servings: 6

3 eggs
¾ cup white sugar
½ cup fresh lime juice
Zest of 1 lime
4 tablespoons butter, melted
½ teaspoon salt

1. Preheat water bath to 170 degrees F.
2. Whisk together eggs, sugar, lime juice, lime zest, butter, and salt in bowl until smooth. Pour into large zip lock bag and seal using displacement method.
3. Submerge in water bath and cook for 60 minutes.
4. Remove from water bath and pour into bowl. Whisk until smooth. Allow to cool to room temperature. Cover and chill in refrigerator for several hours or overnight before using.

Mini Cheesecakes

Cooking individual cheesecakes in mason jars is easy and delicious.

Servings: 6

For the Graham Cracker Crust:

¾ cup graham cracker crumbs

1 ½ tablespoons brown sugar

3 tablespoons butter, melted

For the Cheesecake Filling:

16 ounces cream cheese, softened at room temperature

½ cup white sugar

2 eggs, beaten

½ cup sour cream

1 tablespoon vanilla

Optional topping: Lime Curd (see recipe on previous page)

1. Preheat water bath to 178 degrees F.

2. In bowl, combine graham cracker crumbs, brown sugar, and melted butter. Press layer of graham cracker mixture into bottom of 4-ounce mason or canning jar.

3. Beat together cream cheese, sugar, and eggs until smooth. Fold in sour cream and vanilla. Divide mixture evenly between the jars. Screw lids onto jars until just tightened.

4. Immerse jars in water and cook sous vide for 90 minutes. Remove from water and allow to cool to room temperature. Transfer to refrigerator and chill for 2-3 hours before serving.

5. To serve, top with lime curd (if desired), fresh fruit, or topping of your choice.

Spiced Apples

Try this around the holidays for a sweet and spicy treat.

Servings: 6

6 Granny Smith apples, peeled, cored, and sliced
3 tablespoons butter, cut into pieces
2 tablespoons brown sugar
2 teaspoons lemon juice
2 teaspoons ground cinnamon
½ teaspoon ground nutmeg

1. Preheat water bath to 180 degrees F.
2. Add all ingredients to large zip lock or vacuum bag and shake well to combine. Seal bag using vacuum sealer or displacement method and submerge in water.
3. Cook sous vide for 90 minutes to 2 hours.
4. Remove from water bath and serve hot topped with vanilla ice cream or whipped cream.

Appendices

Beef Temperature Doneness Chart

Doneness	Temperature	Time
Rare	125 F	1 to 2 1/2 hours
Medium-rare	130 F	1 to 2 1/2 hours
Medium	135 F	1 to 4 hours
Medium-well	145 F	1 to 4 hours
Well done	155 F	1 to 4 hours

Lamb Temperature Doneness Chart

Doneness	Temperature	Time
Rare	120 to 124 F	1 to 2 1/2 hours
Medium-rare	125°F to 134°F	1 to 4 hours (2 1/2 hours max if under 130°F)
Medium	135°F to 144°F	1 to 4 hours
Medium-well	145°F to 154°F	1 to 4 hours
Well-done	155°F and up	1 to 4 hours

Chicken Doneness Chart

Doneness	Temperature	Time
Tender and Juicy	150 F	1 to 3 hours
Well-done	165 F	1 to 3 hours

Pork Temperature Doneness Chart

Doneness	Temperature	Time
Rare	130°F	1 to 2 1/2 hours
Medium-rare	140°F	1 to 4 hours
Medium	145°F	1 to 4 hours
Medium-well	150°F	1 to 4 hours
Well-done	155°F and up	1 to 4 hours

Fish Doneness Chart

Doneness	Temperature	Time
Moist, tender, flaky	120°F	45 minutes to 1 1/2 hours
Firm, moist, flaky	130°F	45 minutes to 1 1/2 hours

Egg Doneness Chart

Temperature	Doneness
140 F	Loose and watery white, very runny yolk
145 F	Loose and watery white, slightly thicker yolk
150 F	Opaque, slightly firm white, soft but firm yolk
155 F	Opaque and firm but tender white with firm yolk
160 F	Solid but soft white, firm yolk
165 F	Opaque and firm white, firm moist yolk

Index

A

apples
   Apple Steel-Cut Oatmeal 28
   Spiced Apples 191
Archimedes principle 17
Artichokes Sous Vide 154
Asian-Style Ribs 111
Asparagus with Parmesan 147
avocado
   Shrimp and Avocado Ceviche 135

B

Baba Ganoush 161
bacon 36
bags 15
Basil-Infused Peaches 180
beans
   Hummus 166
   Spicy Bean Dip 165
   Sweet and Spicy Sous Vide Green Beans 150
beef
   Asian-Style Short Ribs 48
   Beef Bone Broth 172
   Beef Medallions in Red Wine Sauce 44
   Caprese Steak Sandwich 52
   Flank Steak with Ginger Marinade 47
   French Onion Meatloaf 62
   Homestyle Meatloaf 60
   Italian-Style Meatballs 57
   Prime Rib with Horseradish Crust 51
   Ribeye Steak with Mushroom Sauce 43
   Smoked Brisket 46
   Sous Vide Burgers 54
   Sous Vide Steak 41
   Steak Tacos 58
   temperature doneness chart 41, 194
   Traditional Pot Roast 63
Blackberry-Infused Gin 176
botulism 18
broth and stock
   Beef Bone Broth 172
   Chicken Stock 171
burgers
   Sous Vide Burgers 54
   Southwest Style Turkey Burgers 96
   Wasabi Salmon Burgers 124

C

canning jars 17
Caprese Steak Sandwich 52
carrots
   Cinnamon-Orange Glazed Carrots 142
cauliflower
   Garlic Parmesan Mashed Cauliflower 151
Cheesecakes, Mini 190
cherries
   Maple Cinnamon Overnight Oatmeal with Cherries 27
chicken
   Chicken Fajitas 91
   Chicken Salad with Mango and Avocado 88
   Chicken Stock 171
   Crispy Fried Chicken 94
   Crunchy-Spicy Chicken Drumsticks 92
   Curried Chicken 84
   doneness chart 194
   Garlic Ginger Chicken Wings 87
   Juicy Whole Poached Chicken 78
   Sous Vide Chicken Breasts 76
   Spicy Chili Chicken Breasts 77
   Teriyaki Chicken Wings 82
   Thai Coconut Chicken 80
chickpeas
   Hummus 166
chutney
   Cranberry Chutney 163
Cinnamon Ice Cream 186
clips 17
cod
   Mediterranean Cod 133
corn
   Cajun Corn on the Cob 152
Cranberry Chutney 163
Crème Brulee, Classic 183
Curried Chicken 84
custard
   Egg Custard 182

D

dips and spreads
   Baba Ganoush 161
   Cranberry Chutney 163
   Hummus 166
   Spicy Bean Dip 165

E

eggplant

Baba Ganoush 161
Eggplant with Spicy Sauce 144
eggs
  Egg Custard 182
  Eggs Arnold 34
  Eggs Benedict 34
  Eggs Blackstone 34
  Eggs Florentine with Baby Spinach 33
  hard-boiled 23
  poached 24
  scrambled 32
  soft-boiled 23
  temperature chart 23, 195
equipment. See tools and equipment
evaporation 17

F

fajitas
  Chicken Fajitas 91
finishing tools 17
fish
  Halibut with Lemon, Coriander, and Scallions 127
  Mediterranean Cod 133
  Seared Tuna Sous Vide with Mustard-Dill Sauce 128
  Simple Sous Vide Salmon 122
  Sous Vide Swordfish 139
  Soy and Ginger Mahi Mahi 136
  temperature doneness chart 195
  Wasabi Salmon Burgers 124
food-borne illness 17

G

gelato
  Hazelnut Gelato 188
gin
  Blackberry-Infused Gin 176
ginger
  Flank Steak with Ginger Marinade 47
  Garlic Ginger Chicken Wings 87
  Honey Ginger Pork Chops 104
  Soy and Ginger Mahi Mahi 136
grains
  Creamy Mushroom Risotto 156
  Spiced Quinoa Pilaf 155
Greek-Style Yogurt 30
green beans
  Sweet and Spicy Sous Vide Green Beans 150

H

Halibut with Lemon, Coriander, and Scallions 127
hard-boiled eggs 23
Hazelnut Gelato 188
Hollandaise Sauce 170

Hummus 166

I

ice cream
  Cinnamon Ice Cream 186
immersion circulators 15
infused olive oil 168
insulated cooler 15
Italian-Style Turkey Meatballs 100

L

lamb
  Easy, Tast Lamb Chops 66
  Greek-Style Lamb Meatballs 70
  Moroccan-Style Leg of Lamb 67
  Rack of Lamb with Garlic and Herbs 69
  Spicy Lamb Kebabs 73
  temperature doneness chart 194
Lemon-Infused Olive Oil 168
Lime Curd 189
Limoncello 175
lobster
  Orange-Poached Lobster Tails 129

M

mahi mahi
  Soy and Ginger Mahi Mahi 136
Marinara Sauce 174
mason jars 17
meatballs
  Greek-Style Lamb Meatballs 70
  Italian-Style Meatballs 57
  Italian-Style Turkey Meatballs 100
meatloaf
  French Onion Meatloaf 62
  Homestyle Meatloaf 60
Mini Cheesecakes 190
mushrooms
  Creamy Mushroom Risotto 156
  Ribeye Steak with Mushroom Sauce 43

O

oatmeal
  Apple Steel-Cut Oatmeal 28
  Maple Cinnamon Overnight Oatmeal with Cherries 27
olive oil
  Lemon-Infused Olive Oil 168
  Sun-Dried Tomato Infused Olive Oil 168
Orange-Poached Lobster Tails 129
Orange-Poached Pears 181

P

peaches
   Basil-Infused Peaches 180
pears
   Orange-Poached Pears 181
pickles
   Zucchini Pickles 162
plastic 17
poached eggs 24
polyethylene 15
pork
   Apple Butter Pork Tenderloin 118
   Asian-Style Pork Lettuce Wraps 113
   Asian-Style Ribs 111
   BBQ Pork Ribs 108
   BBQ Pulled Pork Sandwiches 114
   Chinese-Style Pork Tenderloin 116
   Crispy Pork Belly 112
   Cuban-Style Pork Loin 119
   Glazed Pork Chops with Apricot-Mango Salsa 106
   Honey Ginger Pork Chops 104
   temperature doneness chart 195
potatoes
   Mashed Potatoes with Spicy Brown Mustard 148
   Mashed Sweet Potatoes with Truffle Oil 153
   No Mayonnaise Potato Salad 145
pudding
   Creamy Sous Vide Rice Pudding 185

Q

Quinoa Pilaf, Spiced 155

R

ribs
   Asian-Style Ribs 111
   Asian-Style Short Ribs 48
   BBQ Pork Ribs 108
rice
   Creamy Sous Vide Rice Pudding 185
rice cooker 15
risotto
   Creamy Mushroom Risotto 156

S

safety issues 17–18
salads
   Chicken Salad with Mango and Avocado 88
   No Mayonnaise Potato Salad 145
salmon
   Simple Sous Vide Salmon 122
   Wasabi Salmon Burgers 124
sandwiches
   BBQ Pulled Pork Sandwiches 114
   Caprese Steak Sandwich 52
sauces
   Hollandaise Sauce 170
   Marinara Sauce 174
   Mustard-Dill Sauce 128
scallops
   Sea Scallops with Herb Butter Sauce over Linguine 130
seafood. See also fish
   Orange-Poached Lobster Tails 129
   Sea Scallops with Herb Butter Sauce over Linguine 130
   Shrimp and Avocado Ceviche 135
   Simple Sous Vide Shrimp 134
searing 18
shrimp
   Shrimp and Avocado Ceviche 135
   Simple Sous Vide Shrimp 134
slow cooker 15
soft-boiled eggs 23
sous vide
   advantages of 14
   basics of 12–18
   defined 12
   DIY options 15
   history of 12
   method overview 12–14
   technique 18
   tools and equipment 14–17
   vs. boiling in bag 14
sous vide bags 15
sous vide machines 15–18
spinach
   Eggs Florentine with Baby Spinach 33
steak. See beef
Sun-Dried Tomato Infused Olive Oil 168
sweet potatoes
   Mashed Sweet Potatoes with Truffle Oil 153
swordfish
   Sous Vide Swordfish 139

T

tacos
   Steak Tacos 58
tomatoes
   Marinara Sauce 174
tongs 17
tools and equipment 14–17
tuna
   Seared Tuna Sous Vide with Mustard-Dill Sauce 128
turkey
   Herbed Turkey Breast 99
   Italian-Style Turkey Meatballs 100
   Southwest Style Turkey Burgers 96

Spicy Turkey Legs 81

V

vacuum sealer 15, 17
vodka
  Sous Vide Limoncello 175

W

water bath
  container for 15
  cover for 17
water displacement method 17
water oven 15
weights 17

Y

yogurt 30

Z

zip-lock bags 15
Zucchini Pickles 162

From the Author

Thank you for reading the *Sous Vide Cookbook: Prepare Professional Quality Food Easily at Home*. I sincerely hope that you found this book informative and helpful and that it helps you to create delicious foods for yourself, family, and friends.

Happy cooking!

www.ingramcontent.com/pod-product-compliance
Lightning Source LLC
Chambersburg PA
CBHW042358280426
43661CB00096B/1156